J. P. Wilkinson is a retired nurse, midwife, health visitor and also a lifeguard and swimming teacher. She has cycled around the world and her first book, *Around the World on a Bicycle*, was published in 2016.

I would like to dedicate this book to my late mother, Doreen Rose, who kept all my letters, without which this would not have been written.

J. P. Wilkinson

LETTERS FROM A VSO

AUSTIN MACAULEY PUBLISHERS™
LONDON · CAMBRIDGE · NEW YORK · SHARJAH

Copyright © J. P. Wilkinson (2019)

The right of J. P. Wilkinson to be identified as author of this work has been asserted by her in accordance with section 77 and 78 of the Copyright, Designs and Patents Act 1988.

All rights reserved. No part of this publication may be reproduced, stored in a retrieval system, or transmitted in any form or by any means, electronic, mechanical, photocopying, recording, or otherwise, without the prior permission of the publishers.

Any person who commits any unauthorised act in relation to this publication may be liable to criminal prosecution and civil claims for damages.

A CIP catalogue record for this title is available from the British Library.

ISBN 9781528909105 (Paperback)
ISBN 9781528909112 (Hardback)
ISBN 9781528959155 (ePub e-book)

www.austinmacauley.com

First Published (2019)
Austin Macauley Publishers Ltd
25 Canada Square
Canary Wharf
London
E14 5LQ

First of all, I would like to acknowledge the loving support of my late parents, William and Doreen Grover, who not only gave me their blessing to go and work in Africa, but also wrote to me regularly for the two years I was there.

I also acknowledge the love and support of my brother, Jeffrey; and sister, Stella, who kept in touch with me throughout my stay in Senanga.

I will never forget the people of Zambia, especially those belonging to the Lozi Tribe in Senanga who welcomed and accepted me as one of their own, even calling me "Ma Molisa" (translated as the "Mother who loves the people").

Willie and Dinah Harrington who became my adopted "mum and dad" and made me feel so much at home with them and their family.

The Girl Guides from Senanga Secondary School who taught me so much about "real" guiding.

The Medical Staff at the Hospital, both European and African, who were my "family" for two years.

The Staff of Wigan Library who continued to help and encourage me to write this, my second book.

Last, but not least, my dear husband, John, for his loving support and encouragement over the past two years and his willingness to "proofread" each chapter and actually enjoy doing so!

Foreword

In 1967, whilst doing Part Two Midwifery training at the South London Hospital for Women and Children, in Clapham, I made some enquiries to the Voluntary Service Overseas' Head Office in London.

I explained that I was a State Registered Nurse, having qualified at St. Stephen's Hospital, Chelsea in 1966. I also stated that, later that year, I had passed Part One Midwifery at the same Hospital.

Once I had completed my Midwifery training and become a State Certified Midwife, I wished to serve overseas in my chosen vocation. I really wanted to go to Africa, but I was prepared to go to any of the developing Commonwealth countries, where V.S.O. had their projects.

After a thorough medical examination, the taking up of reliable references and an intensive interview by a panel of six people, I was, much to my immense relief, appointed to go and work in Zambia.

I was sent a description of the project where I would work, which included details of the Hospital and its environment, which I will enclose in this book. It sounded both daunting and delightful!

Before my interview, I had prayed for God's guidance; and I do believe this was given to me quite clearly.

A Bible verse, I still hold very dearly, was of great encouragement to me: Deuteronomy, Chapter 31, and Verse 8, which quotes:

'And the Lord, he it is that doth go before thee; he will be with thee, he will not fail thee, neither forsake thee: fear not, neither be dismayed.' (Authorised Version)

With this written on my mind and heart, I ventured forth into the unknown.

Chapter One
London to Lusaka

It was the first time I had travelled in an aeroplane; thus I was very excited. My only apprehension at the time was that of saying goodbye to my parents and young sister, then aged six, and a few members of my family who came to see me off and whom I would not see again for two years.

I set off from Heathrow Airport on 20th August 1968 and described the take-off as being on a big dipper at Battersea Fun Fair, only you didn't come down again!

It was a comfortable flight; the food was excellent and very plentiful. We stopped at Tripoli to refuel and at 2am it was still pleasantly warm. For most of the time, between bouts of eating, we slept or "dozed". I think we were all exhausted by the effort of continuous digestion!

I remember being impressed by the toilet facilities which were well-provided with various lotions and creams, for both men and women, as well as tissues, cotton wool, disposable towels and individual soaps. These were all by courtesy of B.O.A.C.

I travelled with a young man called John. He was from America and going as a Peace Corps Volunteer to work in Zambia as an agriculturalist. He had studied at college and had practical experience in farming. His work in Zambia would include teaching farming to the Africans, less privileged than him, and helping them to develop their land to its full potential. He would also be teaching the Zambians how to take care of their livestock in order to yield greater reward.

We had some very stimulating conversations during our journey together. We discovered that we were both Christians and also Pacifists. John belonged to a section of the Christian Church known as "Menonites" whereas I was an Anglican.

I had been an active member of C.N.D. since schooldays and John's Church preached Pacifism as one of their tenets of faith. If John had not been a Menonite he would have been conscripted, along with many of his friends, and sent off to Vietnam. Otherwise he would have had to fight his corner as a Conscientious Objector.

John came across to me as a very genuine and humble young man. He told me that for him not to be conscripted was relatively easy as, being a Menonite, he was automatically exempt from combat. He said that he admired the courage and bravery of his friends sent out to fight in such a cruel war and those who had to take the hard stand of refusing to fight at any cost.

I shall never forget John. He inspired me and was an excellent companion throughout our long flight. When we finally landed, we said goodbye, shook hands and wished each other luck. That "young man" would now be sixty-nine years old as I write this, aged seventy-one, in 2016. I do pray that John is receiving God's rich blessings wherever he is now.

There was a second stop at Nairobi; whilst the cabin was cleaned and vacuumed and the crew changed. The weather was noticeably cool and not so different from what we had left behind in England.

Finally we arrived in Lusaka at 12:15 pm only to find that all of us VSO's (12 in all) were debarred from entry! Apparently our work permits hadn't arrived. So we waited nearly three hours, while a British Council official sorted the matter out. We were then split between a jeep and car and taken, via Lusaka, to a Dutch Volunteer's Centre, just outside the city.

I remember very clearly, as we were driven through Lusaka, there being a sharp division between the rich and poor Zambians. The better-off African men were wearing safari suits as were the Europeans. These consisted of short-sleeved shirts worn outside of knee-length shorts, made from blue linen. They also wore long grey socks and smart brown leather shoes. These Zambian men were in the minority, then in 1968, just four years after independence and in contrast with their fellow citizens who were wearing khaki shorts and shirts, often in rags and barefoot.

At first I was rather shocked to see these people in rags; but later I became accustomed to seeing people, especially in the bush, dressed like that. They were obviously well-nourished and would wear their clothes out completely before buying new ones! Also they were adequately clothed for the Zambian climate.

I was beginning to realise, very quickly, just how different this culture was to what I had left behind. Seeing the African women carrying their babies on their backs and breastfeeding quite openly brought this home to me. I was duly impressed, too, by their magnificent posture and ability to carry significant loads upon their heads. I remember thinking at the time how much we in the West could learn from their culture and values.

Arriving at the centre for Dutch Volunteers I was reminded of a typical continental youth hostel such as I had visited several times in Germany and France. We soon settled in and were made to feel quite comfortable.

In the evening we were invited by David (the British Council official, who had met us at the airport) and his wife, to their home for drinks and an opportunity to meet the British High Commissioner, his wife and two Roman Catholic missionary priests.

I immediately took to one of the priests, an elderly Irishman, and we soon became great friends. It was a very pleasant evening, but somewhat tiring. We all wanted just to go to bed and have a good night's sleep. This finally happened at 11:30 pm which was far too late for us travel-worn young people!

We were accommodated in single sex dormitories, with showers and toilets provided, as well as very comfortable bunk beds, in which were soon soundly asleep.

The next morning, on August 22, eight of us had gone their separate ways and just four remained: Diane, a pharmacist; Gill, a nutritionist; myself, and Mick, an agriculturist. We had to wait for further news and contacts to be made with various people who were, supposedly, looking after our interests.

It was arranged for me to meet a United Church of Zambia (U.C.Z.) official and then take a flight, the following day, to Mongu, seventy miles from Senanga – the final destination.

In the meantime, as I wrote my first letter home, we lounged in the beautiful sunshine in a comfortable temperature of approximately 75 degrees, surrounded by brilliant red creeper plants (reminding me of roses) over the walls.

Incidentally, I met Daphne, from Liverpool, whom I was replacing, at Lusaka Airport. She told me she was sorry to go. This was, indeed, very encouraging for someone like me who was at the beginning of a great adventure into the unknown.

Chapter Two
Lusaka to Senanga

Before arriving in Senanga, I stayed in Lusaka for a week. This was because it was impossible for me to get a flight as the connecting airport at Mongu, seventy miles away from Senanga, was closed for repairs.

This proved to be a blessing in disguise: I was able to pick up my excess luggage at Lusaka Airport and also contact the parents of two girls with whom I had done my general nursing at St. Stephen's Hospital in Chelsea, London – Jean and Margaret Burgess.

Whilst in Lusaka I stayed with a family, a Mr and Mrs Rhind and their three children, aged nine, seven and five, who were members of the U.C.Z. and on the hospitality list for anyone working in connection with the Church. During the time I was with them I telephoned Mr Burgess, at the Law Courts, where he worked and was duly invited to share a meal with him and his wife that evening.

Over the weekend I was taken camping at Kariba Dam by the Burgess family – the largest man-made lake in the world. Their youngest daughter, Gill and her brother, John, who was on holiday from boarding school in England, were already there. They had been staying with an American family and their two young daughters.

We had a great time together, sailing, canoeing and swimming. Then on Saturday night we had a barbeque. This was my first experience of one and what a feast we had!

On Sunday I went sailing with Mr Burgess and, to our immense delight, we saw two elephants, a mother and her offspring, coming to the water's edge to drink – not a common sight! I was a hundred miles from Lusaka and I had already seen baboons and hippopotami in the River Kafue, on our way to the

Dam. I had only been in Africa three days, so I was very privileged.

During this "mini holiday" I had time to become acquainted with the pleasant, but nonetheless fierce, tropical Zambian climate and the preponderance of spiders, known as "flatties", forever present on the ceilings and walls of every house! I was, indeed, greeted by these creatures on arrival in my new home in Senanga. I certainly wasn't very happy, having always been afraid of spiders. But there really wasn't much I could do about it!

I finally left Lusaka on Tuesday, 27 August and flew to Mongu on a thirty-two seat "Dakota". This was now my second time to fly, only this was a much smaller aircraft and I was even more excited than the first time.

It was a bumpy flight, owing to the heat and flying fairly low. However, I enjoyed it, but more because it was a new experience than anything else.

I met three British men on board, who were on Government contracts. They were very interested in what I was going to do and wanted to give me a treat before I embarked into the "unknown". I was duly taken to the one and only hotel in Mongu, where I joined these three gentlemen for a sumptuous meal and a pint of lager and lime.

On arriving at Mongu I was met by Jean-Jacques and his wife Christiane, with whom I stayed the night. They were from Switzerland, sent by the Paris Missionary Society, as youth workers, to work for the United Church of Zambia.

That evening we went to see a film – "Stage Coach" – starring John Wayne, showing at the Court House. There was a film flown from Lusaka once a week, so I was there on the right night. Mongu is really only a small town, so that was "painting the town red" for us "Bush" dwellers!

The next day I took a four-seater plane, known as a "Beaver", from Mongu. I sat right next to the pilot and arrived in Senanga after half an hour's very low and immensely exciting flight.

During our journey we were able to wave to all the locals, mostly women working in the fields. Every now and then, Eric, the pilot would give me a wink and then duck the plane down so low that it sent these folk scattering! Aeroplanes here are so rare and the two pilots so well-known that everyone runs out to wave whenever they are right overhead!

I finally arrived in Senanga on Wednesday, 28 August 1968, and was met at the airport by Remi Laedlein, the doctor in charge of the hospital, four miles away. He greeted me warmly and took me and my luggage, which consisted of just one large and one small suitcase, in the hospital Land Rover along Senanga's main "highway" – a broad dirt track road. This was yet another unique experience for me; but the best was yet to come!

Chapter Three
First Impressions

When I arrived at the hospital I was introduced to all the staff, which included the other doctor, Pierre, from France, who had volunteered to work here for a year instead of doing military service. Pierre, his young wife Carmen and five-month-old baby daughter had arrived a few months before me and were just settling in.

I also met Elizabeth, the French nursing sister, and Ann, a VSO nurse and midwife, from England. Ann had almost completed her time of two years and would be returning home in two weeks.

The French staff had all been sent by the Paris Mission Society, which was a Protestant missionary society based in Paris. The Senanga Hospital had been provided by the P.M.S., having been designed by Doctor Annette Casalis, its founder, and built during the Second World War. Zambia was then Northern Rhodesia, and Barotse Province, where we were, was known as Barotse Protectorate and dated back to the reign of Queen Victoria when the Paramount Chief of the Lozi Tribe, known as the "Litunga" was given a special license by Her Majesty to govern the region independently.

Annette was on furlough when I arrived and Remi was in charge in the meantime. Remi had initially served a year for P.M.S. at the hospital, in lieu of Military Service; and then he had volunteered to stay for another two years.

The remaining staff were all Zambian nationals, who had no formal training in either medicine or nursing, but were reliable and very experienced.

I found all the staff very friendly and was given a warm welcome by them all. I remember being quite overwhelmed by the genuine warmth they showed me when I first arrived. It was this which gave me great courage as I faced the tremendous responsibility I was being given as "Sister in charge" of the Male Ward, T.B. and Leprosy Departments, as well as being the "on-call" Midwife during out-of-duty hours, twenty-four hours each day, on alternate weeks.

I prayed to the Lord that He would guide me and give me the strength and wisdom to undertake such duties.

Chapter Four
Senanga Hospital

I started work at Senanga Hospital at 7:30 am the following day, 29 August 1968.

The T.B. and Leprosy Departments were well-looked after by a male dresser on each, both of whom were very experienced and would always call me in any emergency or, indeed, whenever I was needed.

Pierre, who I have already mentioned, was the Doctor in charge of the Male Ward, T.B. and Leprosy Departments. Each day he would do a ward round and, together, we visited the T.B. and Leprosy Departments on a daily basis.

I had two male auxiliary nurses, also known as "Dressers", on the Male Ward. They were called Kayeye and Lubinda and we all got on very well together.

These two young men had been educated as far as Standard Six, which meant they had completed their primary education. Before independence (in 1964) it was almost impossible for the African Zambians to go to Secondary School, especially those who lived in rural areas. Since independence, President Kenneth Kaunda had endeavoured to get a secondary school established in each district of Zambia, which is eight times the size of England. This was a remarkable achievement.

It has to be remembered that the President, himself had only been educated as far as standard six; so, relatively speaking, Kayeye and Lubinda, along with most of the African Staff, were very highly educated for their generation.

When I arrived on the Ward, Kayeye and Lubinda expressed their genuine delight in my being English and not French! This was because English was now the "Lingua Franca" of Zambia and a fluent knowledge of the language was the means towards social mobility. Indeed, much of their spare time was spent studying for the "Form Two" exam by a correspondence course. I helped these two young men as much as I could; but I also encouraged them to develop their nursing skills and consider Nursing as a noble profession.

In fact, over the two years I worked there, I taught the Male Dressers all I knew and, incidentally, lost my Cockney accent in the process! This was also due to the fact that I had to help the French doctors improve their English, especially Pierre and, later on Mark, who each spent a year on my Ward.

I found the conditions in the hospital very different to what I had experienced in England, as well as, needless to say, the patients! I shall never forget the smell, rather, I should say, the stench which first greeted me. Having been a nurse since 1962 I had experienced all sorts of human odours; but this was quite different and hard to really describe. It was akin to the smell of rotting flesh, due to the tropical climate and the very different diseases prevalent in this part of the world. However, I got used to it and, in time, I hardly noticed it

On my Ward there was a total mix of conditions requiring Hospital admission – medical, surgical and orthopaedic – found amongst males, aged from five years old and upwards.

The under-fives were usually admitted, with their mothers, to the Children's Ward. However, if the mother was absent, having, more often than not, died giving birth, the father would be admitted, with his sick young son, to my ward.

Elizabeth was in charge of the Children's Ward and the "Orphanage". The latter was where motherless infants, brought in by either their father or grandparent, were cared for, in residence, until the age of three, when they would be fully weaned and, therefore, on solid food. Had these babies not been looked after they would have died from malnutrition, there being nobody to breastfeed them.

The Zambian female Dressers did a wonderful job caring for these young infants. Elizabeth would sterilise the feeding bottles and make up the formula milk each day and store it in her fridge at her house. She was, indeed, an "Angel from the Lord" although she would never have admitted to this!

I have already mentioned Ann the VSO. She was in charge of the Female Ward and Maternity Unit. Indeed, during the two years she was at Senanga Hospital she had trained two of the

Zambian female Dressers to be "Maternity Assistants". Their names were Anna and Pumalo, very reliable and quite capable of undertaking normal deliveries and postnatal care of both mother and baby.

A few weeks after Ann left, a nurse from Holland (called Elizabeth and known to us all as "Liz") came in her place. This relieved Elizabeth (the French Nursing Sister) and me of the considerable extra responsibilities we had been taking on until Liz arrived to take Ann's place.

Before Liz arrived, Elizabeth and I were on-call twenty-four hours a day, during off-duty hours, for all maternity cases on alternate weeks. Thereafter it would be one week in three for each of us

During my first week on-call I delivered a healthy baby boy, weighing seven pounds and twelve ounces, at 1:50 am. It was a very thrilling experience for me and one I shall never forget.

Chapter Five
My Home in Senanga

I missed Ann very much when she left Senanga, just three weeks after I had arrived. Ann had shared Annette's house and then I lived there for the next two years.

Ann and I became firm friends; we kept in contact the whole time I was in Zambia and we met up again when I returned to England. Ann also contacted my parents when she arrived at London Airport; they met her there and took her home, until she could take her next flight to Bristol the following day.

Ann had her own bedroom, bathroom with a toilet, a small kitchen and a large veranda which stretched along the whole of one side of the house. It had open windows, fitted with wire mosquito netting, along its entire length. During the three weeks I lived with Ann, I slept in the spare bed on the veranda. This later on became my living room and was pleasantly cool all day.

On my arrival and for a few weeks after Ann left, Pierre, his wife Carmen and their five-month-old baby daughter, Zoe, also lived with us. They used Annette's bedroom, bathroom and living room; but we all had to share the small kitchen. This proved very inconvenient, especially for Carmen who had to cook for herself and husband, as well as providing feeds for her baby daughter.

Fortunately, this was only a temporary measure and, well before Annette returned from her leave, a new house had been built for them.

The house in which Remi, the other doctor, lived with his wife, Charlotte and four-year-old daughter, Helene and the one Elizabeth lived in, as well as Annette's, were all built in the traditional Colonial style. This meant they kept cool, even on the hottest of days. They were built in red brick, surrounded by large, leafy trees and always in the shade. There was also a veranda along the side of each of these houses, providing a comfortable living area in the evening and, indeed any time of day.

Contrary to these, the modern houses, although spacious, were not as well-built, neither were they adequately designed for the midday African sun. There were no mature trees surrounding them and they did not have verandas.

I was, indeed, very fortunate to live in the house built for Annette; and I made it my home for the next two years.

Chapter Six
Early Experiences

I wrote my first letter to my brother, Jeffrey, who, at eighteen years old, had just started studying for a degree in Physics and Chemistry at Hull University, seven weeks after I arrived in Senanga. I had been waiting to hear from him and have his news, as I hadn't seen him since soon after he had left school, in July. Jeff had then spent most of the summer holidays hitchhiking with a friend round Europe. He had written before leaving home to go to Hull but I hadn't heard from him since, until receiving his recent letter, sent by surface mail, which had taken five weeks to arrive! I had to understand that he was now a "poor" student!

In my letter, apart from describing all that had happened since arriving in Zambia, I confessed that, for the first time in my life, I actually felt homesick. My new experience was not just one of being "independent", which I had been, since the age of seventeen, when I first left home six years previous. This was different; I couldn't go home even if I wanted to!

I mentioned how much I valued letters from home, especially those from him and my parents. I appreciated very much the "humdrum" news of "ordinary" working-class family life in England. Therefore, letters from my family were very precious indeed.

My new home was situated in idyllic surroundings: from my veranda was a marvellous view of the three-mile-long lagoon which flowed from the River Zambezi. I never got tired of it all the time I was there.

I often swam in the lagoon – crocs, no crocs! And I thoroughly enjoyed the experience. One late afternoon, after a hard day's work, I went down for a swim and, to my great surprise, a group of teenaged, African boys followed me across to the other side. Here they climbed out, running along the riverbank, modestly keeping their dignity, as they did not possess swimming trunks! When they saw me returning to swim back to the other side they soon joined me. And there to greet us were all their mothers, clapping with excitement!

It was sometime thereafter that I came to understand what had happened:

The local people really believed there were evil spirits on the other side of the lagoon and that I, as a white person, had protected these young lads from coming to any harm! In many ways they were right as there had been evidence of crocodiles lurking along the quiet banks of the river plain in recent memory. In fact, about a year after I had been there, a woman came to the hospital, wearing a crude prosthesis to replace a leg she had lost to a crocodile. Remi took no time in bringing it to my attention!

When our water pump broke down, which happened a few times, I would have a wash in the lagoon, along with the local women from the village. They would also wash all their families' clothes, which they put on the bushes to dry while they and their young children washed and bathed in the lagoon. If any men approached this area in their canoes, returning from fishing, they would bang on the side of the boat to warn the women who would then duck down in the water until the men passed by. This was a mark of great respect for their dignity and this part of the lagoon being preserved for the women and children only. The men had their own place further along the bank.

This was actually the best place for me to swim; but, when I did so, I would respect the men's privacy and swim there only when it was quiet, or find somewhere else. This was when I understood more about the culture of these people.

As well as doing the laundry and their ablutions, the womenfolk would also fill their buckets with water, for domestic purposes, and carry them on their head, back to their villages, sometimes up to five miles away. I was in constant admiration of them; this was no mean feat and they worked very hard.

As well as swimming, I used to fish in my spare time, using the doctors' boat, which was equipped with an outboard motor. I was able to catch bream, which was in abundant supply. The Lozi tribe living in Barotse Province were very well-nourished due to this rich supply of high protein, as well as being provided with meat from their cattle.

Eventually, I learned to paddle a traditional dugout canoe, using one paddle only, standing at the end of the boat. This was quite a skill; but, with practise I mastered it and I was, possibly, the first white person, let alone a woman, who had been known to do this! I learned this, a long time later, from the Chief Princess of the Lozi Tribe, who came to stay one weekend with Annette, our doctor. I felt very humbled at the time and quite honoured.

I wrote to my father telling him how lonely I felt after Ann left Senanga. However, there were many compensations: I enjoyed my work very much and made new friends from among the Secondary School teachers at the Boma, i.e. town centre, four miles away. Most of them came from England, so we shared not only the same language but culture also. This became increasingly important when living in the alien, albeit very interesting and much valued, culture of the Lozi Tribe of Barotseland. And, in my case, the culture which surrounded me was very French. I appreciated this too, as I could improve my French, despite learning a lot of slang and swear words from Doctor Pierre! I also enjoyed their marvellous cuisine, whenever we had get-togethers. And, I learned a lot about French cooking, which I was able to put into practise over the next two years!

I also mentioned in my letter just how tired I was as I worked opposite Sister Elizabeth, on call for all the maternity cases, day and night. I had alternate weekends off, consisting of a half-day Saturday and the day off Sunday. However, once the Dutch Missionary Sister arrived in October, our burden was somewhat alleviated and we were each on call one week in three, including the weekend; so I was then less tired. I don't know how they managed when there was only one Sister and one Doctor, in the fairly recent past! The work we did certainly demanded dedication and commitment. But it was rewarding, nevertheless.

At my home there were two hens who laid eggs from time to time, and a black cat, all of which I inherited from the previous VSO. I had never experienced country life before; so this was very new to me and quite refreshing.

The children I met at the Hospital, including the orphans, were not as privileged as even the most poor in England. On my Ward were four ten year old boys: one with a chronic abscess on his back; one with an infected foot; one with severe osteomyelitis; and the other with an above knee leg amputation (caused through gangrene resulting from a snakebite).

They were very happy children despite their suffering; and were absolutely thrilled to bits when I found them three small, toy motor cars to play with.

I wrote to my mother and asked if she could arrange for any unwanted toys, belonging to my sister, to be sent to the Hospital. This was to happen later on; and we would give these as presents to the children, at Christmas.

My mother also initiated the knitting of socks, vests and mittens through her contact with my sister's teacher at the local Church of England Primary School. This kind teacher, Miss Steele was a member of St. Matthew's Church, Ashford, Middlesex, Mother's Union and she got them busy knitting over the next two years!

My mother would parcel up these clothes and send them to me at periodic intervals. Sister Elizabeth was delighted to receive them for her orphaned babies.

My mother also mentioned our needs to a colleague of hers and the local Guide Captain, who was the mother of one of my old school friends. These two good ladies very generously sent appropriate gifts to the Hospital for the children and orphans, from time to time, for the next two years.

Mrs Woodhouse, the Guide Captain, even arranged for her Guides to do a "Good Turn" at Christmas; both she and Kay (my mother's friend) kept in touch with me for the rest of my time in Senanga.

One of the things, strange at first, was how dirty my feet were at the end of the day! If you didn't wash anything else before going to bed, your feet were a must! It reminded me very much of the story, recorded in St. John's Gospel, of Our Lord washing the Disciples' feet. As was the custom in the Middle East, feet would always be washed at the end of the day, due to the sandy soil and the wearing of sandals only. Such were the conditions in this part of Africa which consisted of small shrubs and sandy soil, known as "Savannah".

Where I was living the food was good, wholesome and nourishing, albeit somewhat monotonous at times. Butter could be ordered by airfreight from Livingstone and fresh fish was easily obtained. In fact all I needed to do was to "catch" a fisherman coming up from the lagoon, which was about a hundred yards from our house and buy one from him. A large bream would cost 6d. (2.5p. today)!

There was a market each Monday and Friday where I could buy fresh fruit and vegetables. And we also had a communal garden at the Hospital in which plenty of salad vegetables were grown. Bananas at 6d. a bunch and large papayas at one shilling each were in abundance for most of the year.

The supply of meat wasn't very consistent, especially when there was plenty of fish and the cattle wouldn't be slaughtered. It had to be remembered too, that cattle was still, traditionally, the main form of currency and a man's wealth depended on how much head of cattle he possessed. Brides were still sold to prospective grooms for so much head of cattle!

Beef could be bought for two shillings and sixpence (10.5 p.) a pound. It was all right as long as it was cooked for long enough!

I vividly remember on one occasion, instead of sending my house boy to buy some meat, I went myself and witnessed the animal being slaughtered right in the middle of the dusty track between the Hospital and the nearby village of Litambya! It was a bit gruesome, but quite humane (the animal was stunned before being killed) although not carried out in the most hygienic of conditions.

I was given the honour of being served first with a huge portion of meat, which was passed over the heads of the other bystanders with a shout of "best rump steak for Bo Sisita!"

Incidentally the prefix "Bo" was always used by the Lozis as a mark of respect to all adults and "Sisita" was Lozi for "Sister".

Foodstuff which was homegrown was cheap; but instant coffee, sugar, flour and tinned food, obtainable from the local store (of which there were two in the District) were quite expensive, compared with prices in England at that time.

We also had a meagre supply of eggs from the few chickens we kept; but our hens were very unreliable! I was lucky and was regularly provided with fresh eggs and bread by my white South African neighbour, Marie, with whom I became good friends.

Mealie meal, made from ground maize, was the staple diet among the Lozis. It is a complex carbohydrate, containing some protein and, when cooked, resembles very stiff mashed potato. As an accompanist with any meal it is very substantial. It can also be cooked with more water and eaten with milk and sugar, as porridge, for breakfast.

My "house boy" was an elderly man called "Taulo" – a Lozi word meaning "towel"! So my cooking (breakfast and midday meal), housework, washing-up and laundry were all done by Taulo!

This was very much appreciated, especially as I worked long hours and the climate could really sap your energy. And Taulo received a living wage, for which he was very grateful.

Over the two years I lived in Senanga, Taulo proved to be a "good and faithful servant". I was very sad when it became time for us to say "goodbye"; and I missed him very much.

.

Chapter Seven
Early Days

Our regular working hours were from 8am to 12 noon and from 3 to 5pm. Most often, unless "on call", I slept for an hour in the afternoon, which, I discovered, as time went by, was very necessary to be refreshed and restored.

I would also write the occasional letter; but this, eventually, became something I would do in the evening, when the sun had gone down.

I had a lot of letters to write and was extremely pleased to receive as many as I did. And if I wanted more I had to reply! It was a lot easier to write to my parents, brother and sister, which was something I enjoyed doing. But, as for the others, I had to "pace" myself, as it could become tedious writing more or less the same thing to each person. This, I think, is how most people must feel at Christmas!

I used to go swimming most afternoons and each evening after work. This was something I really looked forward to. I would also meet the local folk and they were delighted that I "loved" their river as much as they did

I would also "have a go" at fishing, from time to time; but I wasn't very successful! Still, I enjoyed trying!

When it was my weekend off, I would finish early on the Friday; and during November I started to lead the Guides at Senanga Secondary School, four miles from the Hospital.

Prior to this the Guides were being "led" by one of the Australian female teachers, who had never been a Guide herself and didn't feel very able, not being equipped for the task.

I used to spend some of my free time visiting the teachers, most of whom were English and married. There was one Russian man, a Pakistani couple, a "coloured" South African (i.e. mixed race), an African couple and two Australian young women.

When I told the latter I had been a Guide I was "roped in" straight away!

Eventually, after writing to Mrs Woodhouse (my friend's mother and former Guide Captain) requesting the Guide Handbook and writing to the Chief Guide of Zambia, I was officially appointed to be the Guide Captain of Senanga Secondary School Guide Company.

Just before I embarked on this, one of the major challenges of my life, I had written to my mother telling her about it. I actually wrote that I didn't feel any more able than my predecessor! However, on a positive note, I said that I might just get them through their "First Aid" and "Swimmer's" Badges! Of one thing I was certain, that the Guides could teach me much more about living in the African Bush (which was our equivalent to Guide camping in the English countryside) and fire lighting than anybody I had ever met.

The Secondary School pupils, some of whom were already in their mid-twenties and older than me, were all boarders. Therefore, they would jump at the chance to get away from school now and again. So I had a golden opportunity to take them camping. As most of the girls were from the rural villages, camping in the Bush was more at home to them than being in the Western culture they had imposed on them at School. For me a new adventure was about to begin.

From October until April we experienced the rainy season and, just before the rains came would be the hottest time of the year, when it was also extremely humid. White folk had even nicknamed it "suicide month", not without good reason I suspected.

I arrived in Zambia with very long, thick hair and was happy to keep it, until October arrived, when I could stand it no longer! I would lie awake at night, bathed in sweat and feeling very uncomfortable. So I had it all cut off! Carmen, Pierre's wife, did an excellent job and gave me a very smart short haircut. What a relief it was!

My male African Staff said it made me look even more beautiful! (Not a description I would have given myself!) This dispelled any fears I had and gave me tremendous confidence.

Chapter Eight
"Imagine No Television!"

The title of this chapter is what I wrote to my brother in 1968. Today it would be "imagine no internet!" I then went on to describe what we actually did for entertainment and how I occupied my spare time.

For entertainment outside the Hospital, there would be a film shown at the Secondary School from time to time. These were very much appreciated; and I enjoyed seeing some good films during the time I spent in Zambia. I didn't go to the "pictures" as often in England; so I was quite satisfied.

In the part of Africa where I lived there was daylight from 6am until 6pm. And when it was dark it was pitch black! All of a sudden, as soon as the sun went down, it was dark immediately. There was no dusk, as we experience in England and, indeed, throughout Britain and Europe.

It took a while to become accustomed to this, as during our summer months the days lengthen and it is light well on into the evening. Whereas in Africa, even with the many days of clear blue skies and sunshine, the darkness coming so early was as if it were winter, yet still very warm.

We had electricity, supplied by the Hospital generator, from 6pm to 9pm. After that we had to rely upon gas or paraffin lamps. I spent most of my evenings either reading or writing letters.

I was very fortunate in having a good supply of books, either belonging to Annette, the Doctor, with whom I shared the house or the schoolteachers, who very willingly provided me with excellent reading material throughout my stay. I avidly read both French and English classics over the next two years, as well as books written by African authors, published by the "African Writers' Series".

After a while I purchased a small, battery operated wireless set and record player. I was unable to get a very good reception on the wireless. Only, very occasionally I would obtain the BBC World News. Otherwise it would be local Radio stations playing African music. I did, however, receive the weekly Airmail edition of the Guardian; and this kept me very well informed.

I bought a few records in Lusaka, when I attended a Medical Conference in December, just a few months after my arrival. I then bought a few more, whenever I had the opportunity on my travels to East Africa and South Africa when on leave; and on one other visit to Lusaka for another Medical Conference during my second year.

When travelling throughout Zambia, Tanzania, Kenya, Botswana and South Africa, during two periods of one month each year, I bought several '45 records of typical music from these regions. This music, representing Central, Eastern and Southern Africa, was really more for dancing to than listening. It went down very well with some of my friends when I returned home!

Eventually, I owned seven LPs consisting of two Beatles ("Sergeant Pepper's Lonely Hearts Club Band" and "The Magical Mystery Tour"), Mamas and the Papas, Gospel and two Classical recordings. The latter were "bequeathed" to me by Brian, one of the schoolteachers, when he returned to England about six months before me, when he had completed his three-year contract. They were Rachmaninoff's "Piano concerto No. 2" and "Theme on Paganini" and Beethoven's "Emperor's Concerto". Brian was a good friend and a great lover of classical music and he helped me to really appreciate it more.

I soon got tired of playing my few pop records over and over again. As much as I liked them there was a limit to how often I could listen to them! However, I would play my two classical L.P.'s repeatedly and loved them more each time. To this day these two musical compositions remain my favourite!

I also spent considerable time using Annette's treadle sewing machine; and became quite expert at making my uniforms and simple cotton dresses. I arrived in Zambia with four white Nurses' outfits and half a dozen summer dresses, which I had made before I left England. In the heat of Africa these soon wore out and, fortunately, I had taken my dress patterns with me; so I could make more!

As time went by I was able to adapt to a life very different from what I had experienced in England and, more to the point, in London where I was born, and where I had lived and worked until coming to Zambia. There couldn't have been a greater contrast between one of the largest cities in the world and the African Bush!

It may have been a "culture shock" at first; but I eventually discovered that living in rural Africa was a much more relaxed and natural way to live. Indeed, the "culture shock" I experienced when returning to England, two years later was far greater!

Chapter Nine
Life in Senanga

The rains arrived a few weeks after my arrival in Barotse Province; and once the banks of the River Zambezi were beginning to spill over, the fishing season would be over until the floods abated six months later. The cattle would now be slaughtered and beef became available.

There were four shops in the District where we could buy soap, toilet articles, tinned food, clothing, cigarettes, and drinks, namely bottled beer from South Africa and fizzy drinks.

Cigarettes were very cheap: 2/6d. (12.5p.) for king-size well-known brands; and even less for those made in Rhodesia, now Zimbabwe) from homegrown tobacco.

Occasionally there would be a party given by Father Lawrence, at the Catholic Mission, to which the Secondary School, Hospital Staff, the Pastor, Rene and his wife, Nicole, and the Boma officials would be invited. Shortly after my arrival there was a party to say "farewell" to two of the schoolteachers who were returning to England.

There was a variety of drinks, plenty to eat and I danced to Western and African pop music until 2 am.! We all thoroughly enjoyed ourselves. Even Father Lawrence, looking like "Friar Tuck" in his habit, shook and twisted like a "good un" for most of the night!

We, i.e. the two Doctors, their wives, and us three Sisters often joined up for meals at the Mission Station where Rene, and Nicole and their four-year-old daughter, Francoise lived. They were from France and had been sent as Missionaries by the Paris Mission Society to work for the United Church of Zambia. The meals we shared were in real French style, with good wine, cognac and even "Gauloise" cigarettes, with good coffee afterwards! These latter items had been brought from France and saved for special occasions.

We would also be entertained at Remi and Charlotte's house with similar fare. We womenfolk all contributed; and I even learned to make mayonnaise using raw ingredients. Sister Elizabeth was a good teacher!

One such occasion vividly remains in my memory when Annette had just returned from "furlough". It was Easter; and on the Day itself (i.e. Sunday) Rene celebrated Holy Communion, in which we all participated; and we sang the well-known Hymn "a Toi la Gloire", which, in the English translation is known as "To Thine be the Glory". We sang it in French, of course. The meal we shared included roast leg of lamb, cooked the traditional French way; it was truly delicious! It was, indeed, a very joyful celebration and one I shall never forget.

At the Mission Station, about three miles from the Hospital there would be an English Service on the first Sunday of each month. And, in the evening of the same day the schoolteachers would be invited, along with the Doctors, their wives and us Sisters from the Hospital; and we played cards and other games together.

One weekend Remi went hunting and brought back plenty of venison, which made a splendid "Fondue Bouguinon" at our house where we used my large veranda for dining.

For this typical French meal the meat was first cut into small cubes and pans of hot oil were placed on gas rings on the table. Each of us put as many of these as we could on long wooden prongs and then dipped them into the hot oil to cook for a minute or two. We then dipped these into various sauces, including homemade mayonnaise with garlic, accompanied with dressed salad. It was truly delicious and, for me a completely new experience.

I often invited Pierre and Carmen to share a meal with me in the evening while we all lived together in the same house. I was a bit apprehensive at first, my guests being French and renowned for their excellent cuisine. However, they always enjoyed my cooking; so I became more confident as time went on.

About six months after my arrival in Senanga, Annette returned from her furlough and, together we would occasionally entertain the hospital staff at our house.

On Boxing Day of my second Christmas, I took courage and invited Sister Elizabeth and Annette to dinner and we had "Canard a l' Orange" (otherwise known as "Aylesbury Duck" in English)!

I had gone into our local village of Litambya and bought a duck from one of the villagers which Taulo, my houseboy, dutifully trussed. Annette gave me a few tips, the meal was a huge success and I was pleased with the result.

I received several cards in time for my birthday on 9th. December, with a letter from my father, arriving on the day itself, and a calendar with pictures of Yorkshire, to remind me of England!

However, I wrote to my parents shortly after, saying, 'I hadn't done much on my birthday. I then went on to say that Pierre and Carmen had sung "Happy Birthday" to me in the morning, and had given me a tea towel with an amazing design of African wildlife. I also made some chocolate ice cream, which I shared with Pierre and Carmen in the evening.

Also, on that day we had an emergency operation in the afternoon – a strangulated hernia – and I had to give the anaesthetic, while Pierre operated. It was my first time and it certainly made my birthday very special. The patient, miraculously, made an excellent recovery!

So, all in all, my birthday was quite eventful!

Chapter Ten
Working Life

During the month of December, 1968 it became quite busy on the male ward of "Litambya Hospital" (as it was called by the local people). I wrote to my brother telling him that we'd had a couple of road accidents (yes, even in the heart of rural Zambia!), one being quite bad. This poor man ended up with a fractured pelvis and femur as well as a ruptured bladder. However, with good nursing care he improved each day and made a good recovery.

This was quite a miracle, taking into account our lack of resources, especially blood transfusions. We had to rely on giving intravenous infusions with dextrose, saline or dextrose/saline at our disposal. Incidentally, I eventually became quite adept at this procedure having previously only observed doctors in England.

The male ward was full, with thirty-two patients; so we were all kept very busy.

It was at this time that Pierre and I visited two dispensaries, each about thirty and fifty miles away. These were visited monthly in order to replenish their stocks of drugs and medication; as well as bringing back any patients who needed hospital admission.

Barotse Province is the flattest part of Zambia and soon it would consist of mostly flood plain, as the Zambezi began to swell during the heavy rains. All the dwelling places were built on large, raised areas of ground, consisting mainly of sand, but with plenty of vegetation. As I wrote about this to my parents I told them that 'everything was as green as England'.

Every district throughout the Province contained many mud hut villages and a "Boma" (our equivalent to "Town Centre"), where all the administrative offices were situated. Here, there were a few shops, a post office, police station and council offices. Our Boma was four miles away from the hospital, Senanga District being about one hundred square miles. Mongu, the capital of Barotse Province, was seventy miles away and, therefore, almost a town; but to call it a "township" would be more correct. They even had a hotel, whereas Senanga had a Government rest house – not quite as grand!

All the main roads consisted of sand and gravel and when it rained it was a lot easier for motorised transport as they became more hard-packed due to the rain.

Pierre and I were away for two days: We stopped overnight at Sefula Mission Station, sixty miles away from our Mission; incidentally, it was at Sefula where Francois Coillard, the first P.M. S. missionary, pitched his tent. The tent peg remains until this day!

There were three British VSO's here at Sefula; and they taught at the secondary school. It was good for me to have their company, albeit for a short time. We enjoyed meeting each other and we had plenty to talk about.

At the dispensaries I had to replenish their stock of drugs, etc. and note what they would need by the next month. The staff at these two dispensaries managed very well, dealing with everything, including maternity cases, as best they could. They were experienced, but not formally qualified. Therefore, although they had the keys to the medicine cupboard, they were not allowed access to it, unless absolutely necessary.

The dispensaries were built in red brick, with corrugated tin roofs, similar to our hospital. There was an all-purpose treatment room, which included a couch, used mainly for maternity cases, a walk-in cupboard for storing linen, bandages, plaster of Paris and an assortment of dressings; and a small side room for the steriliser, surgical instruments, disinfectants and antiseptics. There were also two large cabinets for storing drugs and other medications.

One of the dispensaries, at Nalalo, was right across the flood plain, situated on a small area of raised ground, surrounded by a lake which was fed from the River Zambezi.

Pierre or Remi would go there once a month, accompanied by one of the Sisters. This was my first time; and the first time Pierre had managed to drive the Land rover across the plain without getting stuck in the huge sand dunes situated near the lake. This was because the sand was quite wet; but soon it would be impossible to traverse as it would all be under water!

When we arrived at the lake we had to turn out all our gear from the Land Rover and go across to the village in a "dugout" canoe! It was very exciting (at least for me!) and I thoroughly enjoyed it. On our arrival we proceeded to cook our dinner on a Primus stove at an empty mission house there. We were, understandably, hungry by this time!

It was quite an adventure and one I will never forget.

Chapter Eleven
Preparing for Christmas

Just before Christmas I went to Lusaka, five hundred miles away, flying first to Livingstone and then taking a flight to the capital. I was to attend a Medical Volunteers' course at the University of Zambia, which lasted four days. This was a welcome break; it was good to meet with other VSO's, also doing similar work in the rural areas and to be able to share our experiences.

The course was led by mainly Doctors, many of whom had been Missionaries and quite a few who had been born in Zambia, or, as it was previously known, Northern Rhodesia. Its contents served to refresh and give us new insights into the work we did and the culture we were living in.

Mr and Mrs Burgess kindly met me at Lusaka Airport and took me to their home, where I spent a very pleasant weekend before arriving at the University by the Monday morning. I was also able to see their daughter, Margaret, who was currently training to be a Nurse in London at the hospital in Chelsea, where I had trained. It was really good to see her and we had plenty to talk about!

On my return journey I stopped over in Livingstone for two days and stayed with Reggie and Miriam, a coloured South African couple who were teachers at Senanga District Secondary School. They were spending their Christmas leave there and Reggie's parents and four young brothers had driven all the way from their township in Johannesburg to spend Christmas in Livingstone. We all spent a lovely weekend together, visiting the Game Park, the David Livingstone Museum, seeing a film at the cinema, enjoying a swim in the large open air pool and seeing the spectacular Victoria Falls.

This was the highlight of my visit, being able to see one of the wonders of the world, known as "Mosi o tunya" by the Lozi, which means "the smoke that thunders". What a marvellous occasion it was and such a wonderful experience – one none of us would ever forget!

It was a great privilege to be able to stop with these dear people and meet Reggie's family. It would have been almost impossible for this to happen in South Africa as Apartheid was still in force at that time and would be for another twenty-six years! I was sad to say "goodbye" when it was time for me to leave. However, I knew I would see Reggie and Miriam back in Senanga and Reggie's mum and dad extended a warm invitation for me to visit them when I travelled to South Africa in the New Year. I was determined to do this despite the possible dangers I might encounter.

Before I left for Lusaka I had written to my parents telling them about my plans for the week before Christmas. My mother had written to say she would lay a place for me when they had their dinner on Christmas Day. As I write this I feel quite moved to be reminded of this loving gesture. I wrote saying it would be "like eating with a ghost!" However, "many a jest spoken in truth;" I was with them in spirit after all!

During November, I parcelled up a few gifts for my family. These included an ivory paper knife for my parents, an ivory bracelet for my sister Stella, and one for my godmother's daughter Virginia's 21st birthday, a wild tortoise shell ashtray for my brother Jeffrey, as well as a hard, dried, skin object (which was actually a buffalo's scrotum, given to me by none other than Father Lawrence!) in which to place pens and pencils etc. for his birthday in December, two carved giraffes for my godmother, "Aunty Florence" two carved crocodiles for my Great Aunty Vi, an ivory paper knife for Virginia and her husband, Alan and an ivory bracelet for their little two year old daughter, Natalie. I sent these to my parents, asking them to distribute them; and, thankfully, they arrived safely and were gratefully received.

About two weeks before Christmas I received a card, signed by my sister's teacher, Miss Steele and the whole of her class, including Stella, of course. This was addressed to all the children at the hospital, including the orphans. Stella herself sent me a letter enclosing a picture she had drawn of Father Christmas. It was lovely to receive this as well as cards sent by friends and family and a beautifully wrapped present from a good friend, Ian, with whom I had worked, when I first left school.

I really did appreciate all these loving gestures, especially as I thought I would be very homesick at this time, spending my first Christmas away from England. Much to my surprise I enjoyed celebrating it in a very different way to which I had done previously.

The presents I sent home certainly reflected the differences between the two cultures.

Chapter Twelve
Christmas in Senanga

I arrived back in Senanga on 23rd December, after nine days away, in time to be on duty for Christmas, which I was really looking forward to.

Whilst in Lusaka I did have a "taste" of a more typical English Christmas with the Burgess family. Mr and Mrs Burgess took me, together with their daughter, Margaret and son, John, also home from boarding school in England to see "Toad of Toad Hall" at the theatre in Lusaka. Both Margaret and her parents kindly gave me presents, which I took back to Senanga and opened on Christmas Day. Margaret had even brought a Christmas present with her on behalf of Pam, our mutual friend and nursing colleague, who was still in London, working at St. Stephen's Hospital, Chelsea

So I did have some "family" Christmas festivity after all and it was very much appreciated.

My mother sent a parcel of "old" (i.e. used) clothes, which arrived on my return to the Hospital. Elizabeth, the Sister in charge of the children's ward and orphans was delighted with these and they were put to very good use. The only items that were "redundant" were the socks as I wrote to my mother; "everyone goes barefoot here"! However, Nicole, the Minister's wife was very pleased to have these for Francoise, her four-year-old daughter, as socks were not very easily available in Senanga. Indeed, she said she would welcome anymore should my mother send some again in the future.

I also received some balloons from my mother for the children and these, together with some Ann (the previous VSO) had sent me from Lusaka before she returned to England, made superb Christmas presents.

We had a party for the local children, from the village and hospital, in my front garden, on Christmas Eve. I had painted faces on the balloons and the children were absolutely thrilled with them and thoroughly enjoyed themselves playing, eating bread and jam and drinking orange squash. It was for them a novel experience and very exciting. It was a joy to be with them celebrating our Lord's birth with such simple pleasures

Later on all the Hospital Staff went round the wards singing Christmas carols in Lozi. For me this was reminiscent of the Christmases I had spent at my training Hospital (St Stephen's, Chelsea).Only then we had sung different carols, in English. It was a lovely experience singing with the African Staff in a Bush Mission Hospital.

Much later on the Doctors, their wives, the Pastor and his wife and us three Sisters were invited to the home of Willie and Dinah Harington, a local businessman his wife and four children, who were coloured Zambians and had assimilated both the Western culture as well as the African. We were there until 2am; so we must have enjoyed ourselves! We certainly ate well, sampling both African and European dishes, as well as dancing to the music of both cultures

At 7.30am on Christmas morning, we were all on duty at the Hospital giving out presents to the patients. Later there was a Service, in the open, under a large flamboyant tree, which was attended by the Staff and patients, who were able to walk or, in the case of two women with Leprosy, crawl. This was conducted in Lozi and was a very joyful celebration of Christmas. There was also a bilingual service at the Mission Station to which some us went. This was arranged by Rene, the Pastor and Willie Harington, who both preached in English and Lozi.

With everything that went on I didn't really have time to feel homesick, except for just a brief period around midday when I thought of my family eating their Christmas dinner and wished I could be with them as, indeed, I knew they would be thinking of me! At the time I was sweating in the kitchen, baking mince pies and cakes. This included a large chocolate cake on which I placed a snowman my mother had kindly sent me. It was really appreciated by those, like me, who usually celebrated Christmas in a very different climate.

In the evening we gathered for a traditional French Christmas meal. We had "coq au vin" – chicken roasted in red wine and well-spiced with herbs, garlic and onion (absolutely delicious!), crisp chips, French beans and a roasted leg of lamb, for good measure! This was all "washed down" with an excellent French (of course!) red wine. After this, which was indeed a banquet, a little later on we enjoyed sweets, mince pies, fruit and ice cream, cakes, coffee and liqueurs as well as "cokes" and beers, for those who still had room for more.

Remi dressed up as Father Christmas and distributed our Christmas presents to one another. The children had never seen "Father Christmas" and were a little frightened at first. However, once they started opening their presents their initial fear was overcome by the excitement and joy we all experienced.

Later we sang Christmas carols and had a small service of thanksgiving in French. It was a wonderful occasion and certainly, for me at least, very different from any Christmas celebration I'd had before!

Chapter Thirteen
New Year, 1969

I wrote to my parents on January 4th and told them that on New Year's Day (on which I was off duty) I had gone for a swim in the lagoon just so I could I write and tell them that was what I did! Needless to say I enjoyed it as well, as I always did. I still do today as I write this book in 2016. Nowadays it is known as "wild swimming". It certainly was "wild" in Zambia, where there was the ever-present threat of crocodiles lurking along the riverbanks!

Later, on New Year's Day I visited David and Anna Gould where they held a small party in their humble home. David and Anna were "coloured" Zambians, that is they each had an African mother and a white British father. As such they had blended both cultures like the Harrington family.

David worked as a mechanic for British Leyland. His skills were invaluable. I heard once said that, in the African Bush, qualified nurses and mechanics were like "gold dust", such was their great need. (Doctors would be the "icing on the cake".) Anna, David's wife worked hard as a mother of two young children and running the home.

At the party were Dinah and Willie Harrington and their two grown-up sons, home for Christmas from College and University. We celebrated New Year in style with plenty of home-cooked food and a few beers as well; and we all had a good time together.

David and Anna were then living in a temporary home, made from corrugated iron, while their new house was being built. David told me to write to my parents and tell them I had celebrated New Year in a tin hut!

Chapter Fourteen
Life Goes On

In mid-January I bought a puppy for the equivalent of five shillings (25p). I called him "Toby" and he was the first dog I had ever owned and, as it has turned out the only one, to date! He was a delightful little animal with a mainly white coat with some light brown patches. I had no idea as to which breed he longed to! He was very likely a mongrel as were most of the African dogs. Everybody loved him; and the children from the Hospital would come each day to play with him.

I wrote to my brother, telling him about Toby; I also sent him an African print shirt which I had made for him and ninety cigarettes. These were manufactured in Rhodesia and cost just three shillings (15p.) for a packet of thirty. I never knew whether he ever wore the shirt; but I do know he appreciated the cigs!

I also mentioned in this letter that our mother had suggested that we each bought a tape recorder and sent tapes to our parents. I then added that I thought they would both welcome two years of peace! (Three, in Jeffrey's case.)

We each continued writing letters; but Jeffrey could, of course, visit during his University vacations. However, had I been able to buy a tape recorder, which was very unlikely, my mother would not have had any letters to keep and this book would never have been written.

Chapter Fifteen
Planning My Holiday in South Africa

I had decided to go to South Africa last Christmas when I met Reggie's parents who lived in a coloured township in Grasmere, on the outskirts of Johannesburg. It was when I met them in Livingstone that they invited me to come and visit them.

Also I had a cousin, Vivienne, living in Johannesburg. She was the eldest child of my father's sister, my Aunty Connie to whom I had written to ask for Vivienne's address. Vivienne had been married; but was now separated from her husband and working for an insurance company. I soon wrote to her and she replied to say I was very welcome to stay with her and that she would borrow a friend's car, so she could take me around.

My mother had a cousin, called Bill Bradley, living in Durban, who had settled there after the War ended in 1945. I wrote to his mother, my Great Aunty, who lived in Brentford, Middlesex, to ask for his address; but she didn't have it! However, I was determined to find him!

I also planned to visit Christine, the daughter of Marie and George, my white neighbours, living in Senanga. Christine, together with her husband, Ben, came to visit her parents for New Year; and it was then she had invited me to come and stay with them in Pietermaritzburg in Natal Province, forty miles from Durban.

Christine also gave me some invaluable advice, regarding my travelling arrangements: It was suggested I wrote to the Roman Catholic Mission in Francistown, Botswana so I could stay with them until a lift to Johannesburg could be arranged.

My plan was to travel on a free private flight from Katima, over the border from Zambia, on what is known as the "Caprivi

Strip" and part of South West Africa (now "Namibia"). This flight was ran by W.N.L.A. (Witswaterand Native Labour Association) and regularly flew African labourers to work in the gold mines in Witswaterand. The Africans living in Northern Rhodesia used to go there at one time but when their country became independent in 1964, President Kenneth Kaunda put a stop to it.

The first President of Zambia considered the African labour force to be exploited by the mine owners. I believe he was right. However, in doing so Barotseland (now Barotse Province) lost a considerable amount of income; but sexually transmitted diseases were also reduced!

Already by March the roads from Senanga to Sesheke, one hundred miles away, near the border of S.W. Africa would be impassable due to the floods. The Zambezi had burst its banks and, looking across the plain from where I lived appeared like an enormous sea, except for the odd bits of green shooting up here and there. By May, when I was due to travel to South Africa, the floods would have reached their full height.

I also planned to travel to Paarl, which was thirty miles from Cape Town, where I had been invited to stay with Jenia's mother. Jenia and I had trained as nurses at St. Stephen's Hospital and she had married an Englishman, with whom she lived together with their small daughter in Fulham, London.

I now had quite an itinerary to follow! More about this in another chapter.

Chapter Sixteen
Biking and Guiding

I started working as a Guide Leader with the Senanga Secondary School pupils, early in 1969 each Friday afternoon when I was always off duty; although I would be on call for maternity cases during the night one week in three (now there were three Sisters). This was something quite different from my normal work at the hospital and I found it both rewarding and enjoyable.

It was refreshing to be with these girls, all from traditional rural, African backgrounds, coming from the local villages. They were intelligent and well-educated, having completed Standard Six at Primary School and would become Zambia's first generation of women with such a high level of education.

Their ages ranged from fourteen to sixteen years and it was a privilege to be their Guide Captain and have some influence in moulding their characters for their future and that of their country. My aim was to encourage them to learn from their unique experience of traditional African life as well as to embrace what was of value in the Western culture which was now being thrust upon them

Most important of all I wanted them to know Jesus Christ as their Lord and Saviour and desire to serve God and honour Him with their lives. As their Guide Leader I had the freedom and opportunity to do this more so than their schoolteachers could.

Each week about thirty girls would attend the Guide meeting at the Mission Recreation Hall, about a mile away from the school and four from the hospital. In a few weeks I was already able to enrol one girl as an official member of the worldwide Guide Movement and I was preparing a few more. Soon I would be able to form Patrols and elect Leaders.

I had a letter from the Chief Guide of Zambia sending me her best wishes and the promise of some helpful literature and an application form to be given a warrant as a Guide Leader to be sent very soon. This encouraged me greatly

To add to my encouragement the British Council sent me a Honda motor bike it was a "C.T.90" Trail Bike, especially made for the Bush. It had low ratio gears, much the same as a four-wheel drive range rover, enabling me to ride on the dirt track roads and through the soft sandy soil of the forest tracks.

I had ridden both a Honda motorbike and Lambretta scooter at home, in England on tarmac roads; but never in the conditions had I now experienced. It took some getting used to at first and I was very wary to start with, riding slowly and cautiously, as I was frightened of skidding and "coming a cropper"! However, I persevered and soon I was riding at a fair speed with confidence. And, not once in nearly two years, did I come off, thank God!

When I wrote to the British Council telling them that I had started guiding at the School they had no hesitation in sending me the motorbike as soon as possible. Within two weeks it arrived, gleaming bright in the back of the hospital Land Rover, which had been taken to Lusaka for medical supplies. It was a joy to behold and I was so excited!

The motorbike was truly a "Godsend" as not only did it enable me to travel from the hospital to the Mission Station for the Guides, usually after a long morning's work and often having been up most of the previous night delivering babies; it also meant I could visit my friends at the school the same evening and return home safely when it would be quite dark. Remember, there was no street lighting in the African bush!

I was also able to get out and about at the weekends when I was free; thus I had a much better social life now I had my own transport. It was so much more fun than driving, not that I had a car at my disposal anyway or would have wanted one!

My only other form of transport was the hospital's dugout canoe, in which I could be seen paddling down the River Zambezi on many a weekend! I had long since given up on the Doctors' outboard motor boat, either having run out of diesel or flooding the engine on more than one occasion. When this had happened I'd had to rely on a kind African fisherman to tow me to the bank where I could safely leave my boat and then take me back in his canoe to the hospital, often several miles away!

After these unfortunate experiences and experiencing the wrath of Remi (he was actually quite kind and understanding and saw the funny side of things), I was determined to master the art of paddling a traditional African canoe and I made it my ambition to do so. I used to go down to the river and watch the Africans as they went up and down. Then I decided to have a go.

The canoe was built from a tree and was several feet long, with one equally long paddle with which to steer the boat, standing at one end. It was then possible, with practice, to go from left to right, turn or simply to continue in a straight line.

Being a strong swimmer I wasn't so much afraid of falling into the water, but more so at making a fool of myself. However, I soon mastered the skill and it became a very pleasant hobby, one I enjoyed immensely until it was time for me to leave my home in Africa.

Chapter Seventeen
Decisions!

I wrote to my brother, Jeffrey in February, 1969 whilst sitting in my garden, looking over to the lagoon, which was "beautifully blue, the plain stretching beyond with numerous tributaries meandering across amidst really green flora and foliage".

We'd had heavy down pours of rain every day since October. Most days were hot and sunny, becoming cloudy in the afternoon after which the rain would, quite literally, fall down.

Us Europeans soon became acclimatised to the Zambian weather, it never being too hot. When it rained the temperature would drop to about 75°F., there would be a cool breeze and only then I would put on a cardigan. For the rest of the time I wore cotton dresses and sandals. It was wonderful not to feel cold!

Not only had I adjusted to the climate of Barotseland but life in general, which assumed a regular pattern and routine. In fact I began to consider the possibility serving just one year as a VSO and returning to England in September to train as a Health Visitor. I wondered whether another year would be worthwhile, although I was very happy with my life in Senanga, despite occasional bouts of feeling homesick.

I wrote regularly to my parents each week; but to other family and friends I sometimes had to make a special effort. Although they all thought I had a very exciting life, for me it had become very routine. Just as anywhere, there were occasions which broke the "humdrum". It was at such times that I found it much easier to write letters. It was sometimes difficult to convey my experience of living here in Zambia; so I had to be inspired!

It was during February when Annette, our senior Doctor, returned from her year's furlough. Everyone, especially the local people, were delighted to have her back.

Pierre and Carmen's house was finished just in time, after living in Annette's house for the past six months. They were able to move in the day before Annette arrived! We, i.e. Annette and I, now shared the house together, dividing it in half so we lived separately and could respect each other's privacy. We also each had our own "houseboys" and could supervise the preparation of our meals which they cooked for us every day.

In the meantime Remi and Charlotte were planning to return to France in March; so Annette and Pierre would now remain as our Doctors. The first part of their journey was by pontoon for several miles, due to the floods. It was a very nostalgic occasion when we all said goodbye and sang a hymn in Silozi outside their house.

My father wrote one of his rare letters (it was usually my mother who wrote) and enquired after my progress with the French language. I have mentioned already that English and Silozi were the languages we used at work and socially it would be English and French. However, with the arrival of Harry and Marjorie (an elderly retired couple from Canada) we spoke more English. I did listen to a lot of French over the two years, which resulted in my being able to read many of Annette's books which were mainly French classics; so some of it must have sunk in!

I had planned to visit South Africa in February, but decided to defer this holiday until May, so I could go to the Kuombuka in March. I was so pleased to have made the right decision as everything then fell into place.

I would always pray about important decisions and I certainly did experience the Lord's guidance. Reflecting over the years I can see this clearly, and I pray more often now!

During April, Pierre was going to relieve an elderly missionary Doctor in Mwondi, near Livingstone, so that she could come and stay with Annette for a few weeks' rest. Therefore, were I to go to South Africa then, we would be very short of qualified staff at the hospital; thus, my decision to take my annual leave in May.

Another, even more important decision I made was to stay in Senanga another year. I had a talk with Annette, who certainly did not persuade me to stay; but she did encourage me by saying that I would be much more useful by staying. As she pointed out, in one year they would have just got used to me and then I would be off, without making a real impact, which was what had happened with the previous VSO.

The day I made this decision, I started training Siumbwa, who was a cleaner on the Male Ward. Siumbwa showed great promise. He was an intelligent young man, hardworking and conscientious. I could always rely on him to do a job well; so, on my recommendation Annette agreed to my training Siumbwa as a medical orderly. This would take a year. It confirmed my decision and made it seem so right for me to stay. And I'm glad I did!

As for Siumbwa, neither I nor Annette ever regretted our decision, and he proved to be a very reliable and valued member of the male staff.

Chapter Eighteen
The Kuombuka

In March, 1969 I attended a big ceremony in Barotse Province, known as the "Kuomboka". It was the moving of the Litunga (the equivalent of the King of this part of Zambia) from his dry season home to his flood time home.

When Northern Rhodesia existed, Barotse Province was then called Barotseland and was a British Protectorate. As such, it had always had a king as it was a separate country; but when Zambia became independent, in 1964, it was forgotten by the British Government.

A treaty had been signed by Queen Victoria during the 1890s and it still existed. Although Barotseland was now a province of Zambia, it still retained its traditions.

The late Litunga died in November 1968, and Remi, our senior Doctor at the time, attended his funeral. As there was now a new Litunga, it promised to be a very spectacular celebration.

I had already visited the palace of Princess Nalolo, the Litunga's daughter, where we had a dispensary; but I did not see her at the time. However, I did have the privilege of meeting her when she came to stay with Annette the following year.

Thus, in mid-March I travelled in the hospital Land Rover with Pierre and Carmen and several other people from Senanga Secondary School. We all "piled" in the back; there were nine adults and two children, with not a lot of space between us! Off we went to Sefula, sixty miles away, where we stayed at the Mission Station for two days. This was so we could take part in the "Kuombuka", a ceremonial occasion when the Paramount Chief (known by the Lozi as the "Litunga") moved from his palace on the flood plain to his winter palace in the forest. It was actually broadcast on BBC Television on Sunday 16 March on a programme called "Twenty Four Hours".

The Kuombuka was a very traditional and colourful ceremony. We first went to Mongu, ten miles from Sefula; and eleven of us got into an especially hired barge, which took us along a non-existent canal (the plain being flooded) for about fifteen miles to the village of "Lea Lui", the home of the Litunga's "summer" palace. This was surrounded by water, with only a little dry ground around the palace itself. Apparently the Litunga moves as soon as he gets his feet wet! Only then can the remaining residents move too, which they did, in their dugout canoes and all their belongings tied up in cloths!

The Litunga's barge was magnificent, about fifteen yards long and painted with black and white stripes. There was a canopy in the middle, where the Litunga sat, along with thirty paddlers, dressed in lion skins and several drummers on board.

The crowd of onlookers consisted mainly of Africans, including several local dignitaries and quite a few Europeans. Incidentally, the Africans dressed in suits and ties, were much smarter than the white folk, who wore either shorts or simple cotton dresses. We were also bare foot, as we had to climb out of our boat and wade through the water to reach the palace!

When the Litunga came out of his home, dressed like an English gentleman in a pinstriped suit and bowler hat , to board his barge, there was a procession of people, walking in front and behind, carrying all his belongings. The music from the African drums was wonderful, and we all knelt down in typical Lozi fashion as a mark of respect as he walked past us.

After seeing the Litunga embark on his journey across the flooded plain, we went for a hot meal at the Mongu Hotel, where we managed to dry out and warm up. Unfortunately, Carmen, Pierre's wife, who was ten weeks pregnant, started to miscarry, probably due to the bumpy ride in the Land Rover the previous day. We rushed her to hospital, which, thank goodness, was very close by and she made a good recovery, staying in hospital just three days.

We left the hotel, now replenished, and Pierre took Jeanette, her four-year-old son, William, Brian and myself in the Land Rover to Limulungu. This was where the Litunga's barge would arrive and where his winter palace was situated.

There were large crowds there and it was wonderful to see the barge arrive, with the beating of drums and the people dancing and shouting joyfully. There were also many primary schoolchildren, dressed in bright new uniforms, beating drums and marching up and down, carrying their respective school banners, singing at the top of their voices!

There were too many people for us to see the Litunga walk up to his palace; but we'd had a good view that morning at Lealui. Also, we weren't able to push our way through the crowds as little William was complaining of being squashed as it was! (Bless him)! However, Jeanette, the wife of one of the secondary school teachers and also the School Matron, and I found a lorry and we climbed up onto the top of the cab from where we had an excellent view of the palace forecourt.

Privileged Europeans, such as the Limulungu Missionaries and the Roman Catholic Priests and nuns were allowed inside; and, of course, the Zambian dignitaries.

We didn't see a lot more, except loads of schoolchildren, marching round in circles. I enjoyed this spectacle very much; but Jeannette and Brian, an English chemistry teacher at Senanga Secondary School, said they saw schoolchildren every day and that was enough!

However, we all appreciated the magnificent view of the Litunga's palace, which was quite elaborate and made from whitewashed clay. His summer palace at Lealui was built from mud bricks and grass with a thatched roof, in the traditional rural African style.

We left these celebrations and proceeded to visit Pastor Andre Honiger, working for the Paris Mission Society, his wife, Jacqueline and their four children, living in Limulingu, close to the Litunga's palace. We were given a very warm welcome, with Jacqueline making endless cups of tea for everyone who came to their home that day. They lived right off the beaten track and were really pleased to have some visitors.

Reluctantly we left Limulingu having been completely refreshed and rested, and returned to Sefulu where we spent the night with the two VSO's working there. The next day we set off for Senanga. What a journey! The roads were all dirt track and very bumpy. On arrival we were quite exhausted!

Carmen flew back from Mongu a few days later, safe and sound and much rested, by which time we also had recovered!

What wonderful memories we all had to treasure.

Chapter Nineteen
Minor Setbacks

In February, my little dog, Toby, died quite suddenly at the age of just two months. He started being ill two days beforehand; so I gave him Penicillin injections and kept him warm. He seemed to improve later on that day, but by the next day he became rapidly worse and died at midday. I think he must have had Distemper for which, at that time, there was no vaccination. However, he had been vaccinated against Rabies, so that, at least, could be eliminated as a cause of his death. I really missed him at first and thought about getting another dog; but eventually decided against this.

During March I had my first bout of Malaria, potentially a very serious, even life threatening illness, especially for a European. Malaria is endemic in Zambia; therefore the Africans do have some immunity, so that when they contract the illness it is in a much less serious form. The main threat to them is the increased risk of developing Sickle Cell Anaemia, which is, of course, very serious.

I wasn't sure what to expect when I first became ill. However I did feel different from any other illness I had ever had which resulted in a fever. I was on duty at the time and very suddenly I was full of aches and pains and felt quite ill. I carried on until I finished the morning shift at noon, and, without having anything to eat I went straight to bed.

Within a very short time my temperature rose from 99 degrees F. to 101, eventually reaching 103 degrees. I stayed in bed for two days; and, in the meantime, my dear houseboy, Taulo, brought me in black tea with sugar and Annette administered injections of Chloroquine twice a day.

As my temperature rose, I felt freezing cold and couldn't stop shivering and needed an extra blanket. The following day, as my temperature gradually started to drop, I had completely soaked my bedclothes and felt very weak.

Liz, the Dutch Sister, kindly changed my bed for which I was very grateful. By Monday I was back at work. I hadn't had to take any time off as it was my weekend free! Although I returned to work so soon, it took me some time for me to regain my appetite and gather strength. I don't think I would survive so well now!

My spirits lifted on the arrival of Easter. We had a lovely Good Friday service of Holy Communion in our house, conducted in French and English by Renee, our Pastor. Prayers were said in both languages and we sang French Hymns, including "A Toi la Gloire" ("To Thine be the Glory").

There was also a bilingual (Lozi and English) service at the Mission Station on Easter Day; unfortunately, I wasn't well enough to attend.

Not long after I had recovered from Malaria, I was paid a visit by the Director of Voluntary Service Overseas from England, where he worked. He was visiting all the VSO's in Zambia and I felt very privileged to meet him. He came with a representative of the British Council in Lusaka and they shared a meal with Annette and me. It was a "flying visit", literally, but very worthwhile. Both gentlemen were very pleased to find me so happy and well-settled in Senanga. I was able to write and tell my parents this; thus they were reassured. I did make light of my illness though, so as not to worry them unduly.

And I thanked God for my return to health and a full recovery.

Chapter Twenty
A Trip into the Bush

My neighbour, Marie, who lived with her husband, George, in Senanga, both of whom were white Africans, was due to arrive in Katima, on the Caprivi Strip. She had been on holiday with her daughter in South Africa and was flying from Francistown in Botswana.

George had arranged for me to go with one of his drivers to meet her and I was going to take the opportunity to "speed up" my flight arrangements in Katima for when I travelled to South Africa in May. I hadn't heard anything definite yet about my flight to Francistown. I also needed permission from the South African authorities to enter the Caprivi Strip, which was part of South West Africa, belonged to South Africa and separated Zambia from Botswana.

We duly left Senanga one Wednesday afternoon in April (I was given time off to do this) in the Land Rover, travelling by pontoon (a motorised floating bridge) for the first twenty miles owing to the floods.

About five miles from our destination, the engine broke down and, as it was just getting dark, we all slept out. The only females were myself and two young girls from the Secondary School. The two schoolgirls and I slept in the Land Rover on a large mattress on which we were quite comfortable, whilst the men slept outside.

The following day we were up with the sun at 5am. The men made paddles out of planks of wood and eventually we managed to reach Nangweshe on the other side of the flooded River Zambezi

When we arrived there, one hundred miles from Katima, we discovered from one of the locals that Marie had been able to get a lift and then a special boat, early that morning and was already on her way to Senanga! We didn't see her pass us because they had taken a different route across the flood plain and not via the main river.

I was quite fed up by this time, compounded by the men wanting to drive off somewhere in order to buy sugar! I didn't want to waste any more time; so I collected my things, went back to the riverside and managed to wangle a lift on the District Secretary's boat, which was shortly arriving for petrol, the lack of which was the cause of our Land Rover breaking down!

I spent the best part of the day travelling up the River Zambezi on a motor boat "cooking" in the sun!

Eventually I arrived back at the Hospital that evening with nothing gained but a lovely suntan!

George was furious that the men didn't continue their journey and take me to Katima. However, everything worked out for the best, because, when I arrived back, there waiting for me was a letter regarding my flight, saying that as soon as there was a space on the plane they would inform me.

The next day I had the chance to accompany a patient from our hospital to Mongu, where he could receive the treatment he required. Thus I was able to go to the Bank and obtain Travellers' Cheques for South Africa. These were absolutely necessary as it wasn't possible to take Zambian money out of the country and there would have been very little chance of me being able to go to Mongu before the end of the month, and I was travelling to South Africa in May.

I was also able to go to the dentist and have a check-up requiring a small filling. Again, this was a "Godsend" as the dentist was due for a transfer soon after!

Another blessing was being able to visit Gill, a VSO Nutritionist, for a meal that evening. And, beforehand, I had joined the Nurses at Mongu Hospital for their afternoon tea break. They even had a box of chocolates; but, as the dentist was with us, I had to abstain!

Chapter Twenty-One
The Litunga's Visit

During April 1969 the Paramount Chief (King) of Barotseland, otherwise known as the "Litunga", visited Senanga. It was very exciting:

He arrived in his barge with all the paddlers, along the river, passed nearby the Hospital and landed at a village two miles away. It was my half day off, being Friday; so I got on my Honda motorbike and rode up to Dinah's and Willie's house near Mufalo Village, where the Litunga spent the weekend.

The Hospital staff came in their Land Rover; and as there were so few Europeans present, the occasion was much more traditional and realistic than the Kuombuka had been in March, which had become a tourist attraction.

The Litunga disembarked and walked slowly up the paths to the sound of drums, wearing an Admiral's suit which had been presented to an earlier Paramount Chief by Queen Victoria. All the men and women danced for him as he arrived at the village.

On Saturday afternoon, the next day, he visited our Hospital dressed, this time, like an English gentleman. We were all very excited; and the African staff simply thrilled to bits, as this was the first time for many years that the Litunga had visited the Hospital.

All the local villagers turned out and there was a host of people all along the path from the river to the Hospital as well as lining the banks.

He came round to all the wards followed by three important people. Each Sister was introduced to him and I showed him round my Ward. He was aged about sixty and spoke excellent English, having been educated at Oxford University, where he had obtained a degree.

Previous to him coming to my Ward, Annette had escorted him from his barge to the sound of drums and I had followed behind! I then had to return quickly and get all my patients back into bed in time before the Litunga arrived! Fortunately he visited the Female Ward first!

Afterwards the Litunga came to our house for tea. All the expatriate staff and a few of the male and female Zambian nurses were invited. However, there were crowds of people in our garden outside!

After tea the Litunga and his entourage went back to Mufalo; and, on Sunday, he spoke at the Church service at the Mission Station where he had tea later on in the afternoon. I was unable to attend as it was my weekend on duty.

The following week we had another important visitor, the Provincial Medical Officer of Barotse, an African from Mongu. So, in two weeks we'd had some distinguished guests. We would probably not see anyone for months now!

Chapter Twenty-Two
My First Trip to South Africa

Part One: The Journey to Johannesburg

On 6 April, 1969 I set off on my journey to South Africa via the Caprivi Strip (in what was then South West Africa and is now Namibia); and Botswana.

I couldn't wait any longer to hear from W.N.L.A. (Witswaterand Native Labour Association) to know whether or not I could fly with them to Francistown in Botswana; so off I went!

I was unable to get a flight at Senanga Airstrip, but managed a lift on the Forestry Department's speed launch across two pontoons, on the River Zambezi to Nangweshi, where I was very fortunate to get a Land Rover for one hundred and twenty miles to Katima, on the border of Zambia and South West Africa, where I spent the night in a rest house.

The next morning I walked across the border onto the Caprivi Strip, where the first European I met just happened to be a Mr Japp, none other than the W.N.L.A. Rep.! I was thereupon invited to his home and given a "slap up" breakfast, after which I was taken to the Aerodrome, where I boarded the plane to Francistown. I was truly grateful for all the kindness I had received over the past two days.

I sat on the plane, at first on a crude wooden seat surrounded by African labourers, who seemed very pleased to have me as their travelling companion. Although uncomfortable, I was quite happy to be with these delightful people. However, I was "rescued" by the co-pilot and taken into the cockpit for the remainder of the journey, which was quite exciting with marvellous views of the African panorama below.

At the airport, I was soon met by the Priest from the Roman Catholic Mission, where I was given excellent hospitality. I spent most of the next day either sleeping or eating and being entertained by the Father and Brother.

That evening the chief Priest, Father Germanous, a great Irish "bloke", returned from his missionary travels and fixed me up with a free lift on a flight with Botswana National Airways, upon whom he must have had substantial influence! In fact, he had a friend working for them!

The next day, I departed from Francistown early in the morning and flew the five hundred miles to Gaberone, the very modern capital of Botswana, where I was met by a Mrs Lowry, the wife of the Commissioner of Police (a good Catholic family, and friends of the Fathers in Francistown). I was given a lovely meal in the home of these good people and then driven to the Border Gate, thirteen miles out of town. Here I was able to get a lift to Johannesburg, four hundred miles away, with a very nice man with whom I felt quite safe, as was always the case whilst in South Africa.

We eventually arrived in Jo'burg and I was taken to my cousin Viviane's address at 7:30pm; and to my surprise, we found her in! As she was something of a night bird this was very lucky for me.

It was great to see her after several years when we had both been young children. We got on immediately like a "house on fire" and, soon after my arrival we went, together with Viviane's friend Quintin, to a steakhouse where I "polished off" a T-boned steak, something I had never had before.

The whole meal cost just one Rand, which was ten shillings in England then and now 50p. The cost of living in South Africa was a lot less than in Britain; and the wages were much higher; thus the people (at least the whites) had a very high standard of living altogether.

It was much colder here than Zambia, just like our autumn, as it would be in late October. For the first time since leaving England I was wearing skirts and jumpers and stockings and shoes, instead of simple cotton dresses and sandals.

On the Saturday night we were taken out by George, a single middle-aged man from London, with whom Viviane worked, to see a very good film, "The Fixer". Afterwards we went to the

25th floor of the "President Hotel" from where there was a magnificent panoramic view of the city in twilight. We had a drink in the posh bar before going on to the "Tulip Room" in the Rand International Hotel, for a terrific meal with wine etc. I had duck with orange sauce – again a first, and extremely tasty. I also had a starter consisting of frogs' legs in garlic sauce; it was delicious!

On Sunday George drove us to Pretoria, the capital of South Africa, thirty miles away where we visited various sights. This is, indeed, a beautiful city, set among the hills with large gardens everywhere.

We had coffee and scones at a classy hotel set among the hills; and later on we went to a smart bar for drinks. As I wrote to my parents, "I ate like a king" after a monotonous diet of Barotse beef and rice! It was great to be back in "civilisation" again, so I thought then, when I wrote my letter home.

Part Two: En Route to Cape Town

Viviane, my cousin, put an advertisement in one of the local shops in order to secure a lift for me to Cape Town where I had planned to stay with my friend Jenia, with whom I had done my nurse training at St. Stephen's Hospital in Chelsea. Jenia came from Paarl, a small town, about thirty miles away from Cape Town, in the wine growing area of Cape Province. She now lived with her husband, Tony, an Englishman and their two small children in the city of Cape Town.

Within two days of the advertisement I was contacted by a kind gentleman who was travelling to Cape Town on business the very day I was planning to leave Johannesburg.

Reluctantly, I said goodbye to Viviane and left Jo'burg where I had spent a very enjoyable and eventful week; and I travelled the thousand miles to Cape Town with a businessman called Paul, who came from Port Elizabeth, on the East Coast. He provided very pleasant company and, being an Afrikaaner, whose ancestors were the Boer farmers coming from Holland some three hundred years ago, he was very interested to meet an English girl from London who had mixed freely with different ethnic groups there, had many friends from among them and was now living and working amongst black people in the African bush. What was more; Zambia had an African President, namely, Dr Kenneth Kaunda.

I discovered through our many stimulating conversations that Paul was not at all racist, but just had not enjoyed the experience of freely mixing with Africans on an equal level. He had been brought up in a very repressive regime and had only known Africans as servants, but not as friends and equals. He sincerely hoped that one day Apartheid would be abolished and that both Africans and Coloureds would be given the same opportunities as the Whites. Of course, this was to happen twenty-five years later. I only hope Paul lived to see this happen as indeed, I had.

An interesting experience was during our journey along the "Garden Route" (on the East Coast of Cape Province). Paul insisted I accompany him to visit his very elderly mother living on a farmstead en route.

Paul's mother was delighted to see her son and to meet me. We were served with tea and homemade cake and given a warm welcome. As we talked together and this lovely lady, a devout Christian, learned more about me – my background and my present work in rural Africa (especially Zambia, an independent democracy) she was amazed. She said I was a very brave girl to live and work in such a place!

When we resumed our journey after a very pleasant visit, Paul explained why his mother had reacted in such a way. She was old enough to have lived through the Zulu War and remembered well the horrors she had experienced at the time. This was a revelation and helped me to gain more insight into the average Afrikaner's mind-set, something many critics of the Apartheid would find hard to understand, especially those from overseas.

I stayed with my friend Jenia and her family in Cape Town for five days. It was good to see her after two years since we were both in London together, working at the Hospital. We were able to catch up on all our news.

Tony, her husband, had a job as a sales rep. with Olivetti in Cape Town; hence their being able to come and live there. However, the longer I stayed with Jenia I could tell she would prefer to go back to England which she now regarded as her home.

Jenia's older brother, Peter, had already left South Africa several years previously and did not wish to ever return to live there, mainly for political reasons. I was able to see him when I returned to England, primarily to give him news of his mother, Jenia and his niece and nephew; and to take him some presents. I was impressed by his sincere convictions, which he held so dearly.

One day when Jenia was working at the local Hospital I visited Paarl, a beautiful small town, surrounded by mountains; and I visited the biggest winery in the world. I was able to do some serious wine tasting (very enjoyable!) and obtained a free cookery book for wine recipes. I didn't have much use for it in Zambia. I also purchased a bottle of sherry, which I took back with me for "special" occasions – much more useful!

I travelled to Paarl on the local bus and, as a white person, could only get certain buses. I had to wait some time for one, during which several buses full of laughing, joyful Africans went by; and, not only would I have made my journey in less time, I would have been happy to travel with them.

On the "white" buses "Coloureds" were allowed; but they did not mix with us. However, I sat next to a coloured lady and tried to make conversation, but she was not very responsive. When we both got off at our destination I asked her where I should go to get to the winery. She pointed me in the right direction, which included crossing a small river by a footbridge. As we approached this bridge I naturally followed the lady and she appeared alarmed and moved away from me. What I had not observed was that the bridge was divided into two sections, one for whites and one for non-whites; and I was going to cross on the "wrong" side!

I began to really feel Apartheid affecting me; but I realised how much worse it was for the non-whites in South Africa. Thank God this is not the case today.

One of the days I spent in Cape Town was with Jenia, on her day off, when we travelled to Camps Bay and climbed Table Mountain – on the cable car, I hasten to add! The scenery was magnificent. I didn't know at the time that I would return in forty years' time and cycle round this area and climb the Lion's Head, a nearby peak!

We also visited Jenia's mother in Belleville, fairly close to Paarl, where she had a shop stocked with bridal gowns and hats which she had made herself. She was a lovely lady and I thoroughly enjoyed her company. I was even invited to go and live with her when I had finished working in Zambia! A year later I was able to visit her again, on my way back to England.

Part Three: A Visit to Durban

By the time I left Cape Town I had already travelled two thousand five hundred miles since leaving Zambia; and, as I wrote to my parents, I was beginning to Miss Senanga and the African bush. "It somehow gets you."

I was discovering that South Africa, having been so heavily influenced by Western European culture, wasn't "Africa at all" and that "Africa itself was something quite different". Really this has to be experienced first-hand to be understood.

I left Cape Town to hitch-hike the one thousand one hundred miles to Durban and succeeded in getting a lift for three hundred and fifty miles, along the East Coast, where I met a young man, Lee, who was visiting his parents in East London. We stood on the road until 9.30pm; and then called it a day.

We decided to enquire at the nearest hotel for the local Police Station, where we hoped we would be given shelter. To our surprise the manager kindly gave us a room each, free of charge; and regretted we had to share the bathroom!

The following evening we arrived in East London, where I stayed the night with Lee's parents, who were originally from England but had lived most of their lives in Kenya. The next morning Lee's mother packed me some sandwiches and her husband put me on the road for Pietermaritzburg where I was able to stay with Christine and Ben (the daughter and son-in-law of Marie and George in Senanga).

The next day Christine and Ben put me on the road to Durban, on their way to work; and I was there by 8:30 am!

On my arrival at Durban my driver very kindly took me to the National Party's Office where they were able to obtain my mother's cousin Bill's address. I was then taken there where I left a note to my relatives explaining who I was and informing them as to where they could find me.

I thanked the kind gentleman, who had been so helpful and proceeded to the nearby beach, where I spent the rest of the day sunbathing and swimming in the sea, at long last. I had been looking forward to this ever since arriving in South Africa. It had been much too cold and dangerous to swim off the coast at Cape Town.

Whilst in Cape Town I had looked in a telephone directory for Bill Bradley's address and had found one listed under a W.R. Bradley and then sent a post card to inform them of my arrival in Durban within the next few days. I later found that "Uncle" Bill's phone number was listed at the Party Office in his wife's name. However, my determination to find my mother's cousin was eventually rewarded and I truly thanked God.

I phoned Uncle Bill at 5:30 pm when I assumed they would be home and they all came to pick me up; i.e. Bill, his wife Cath, and Diane, their daughter. I was duly made very welcome at their flat and it was good to meet members of my family for the first time. Uncle Bill, who was roughly the same age as my mother, had served in the Royal Navy during the war and visited South Africa whilst on service. He fell in love with the country and promised himself to return, which he did with his wife Cath; and together they made their home here and raised their family, Diane and their son David.

David had his own flat near the beach and worked for the Government as a professional diver. He was very fit and a keen surfer. He came round to meet me later on that evening and very kindly gave me keys to his flat so I could use his surfboard. I duly went each day to the beach, while the rest of the family were at work, and try as I may, I was unable to surf. Certainly I wasn't afraid of the water or the waves; but the surfboard was far too big and heavy for me to handle! I confess I gave up on the first attempt!

However, I thoroughly enjoyed swimming in the Indian Ocean and relaxing in the sun on the beautiful golden beach each day of the week I spent in Durban. I was also able to shed my warmer clothes and wear my summer dresses and sandals once more, which was a blessing.

Diane was five years younger than me. It was great meeting her; we shared her bedroom and got on very well together. Uncle Bill and Aunty Cath took me out most evenings and I had an evening out with Diane and her friend. We went for a meal and then on to dance at a psychedelic teenage "joint". We all thoroughly enjoyed ourselves, despite Diane and her friend thinking they were too old for it!

I still found it strange to be mixing with only white folk. Even in England and especially in London, where I was born and had lived all my life, this was never the case. There was always an ethnic mix wherever I went; and in Zambia this was even more enhanced, as we expatriates were very much in the minority.

One special occasion was when we all went to a "Drive-in movie" to see "Taming of the Shrew" with Elizabeth Taylor and Richard Burton. It was a magnificent film and true to the Shakespeare script. (In South Africa what we colloquially call the "pictures" is known as "bi-scope".)

This was to be my last stop before making my way back to Senanga; and, indeed, it was a memorable one. Being able to meet members of my own family, for the first time, so far away from home and get to know them so well, meant a great deal to me. It was, therefore, with mixed feelings that I said "goodbye" the next morning, when I set off on my journey back "home".

Part Four: Returning "Home"

I left Durban, sad to leave my "new" family, but happy to be going back to work in Senanga. As I wrote later to my parents, South Africa is fine for a holiday. Indeed it is a very beautiful country. However I had fallen in love with the authentic Africa, which is where I lived for two years.

In Senanga, I experienced traditional, rural African life and I didn't want to swap it for anything, except my home in England, where I really belonged.

I hitched a lift with a kind businessman; and was taken the four hundred miles to Johannesburg. Here I was able to contact George, my cousin Viviane's friend from London. He was a real gentleman and looked after me like a "Dutch Uncle". The evening I arrived, he took me out to the Rand International Hotel for a fabulous meal of fried trout and all the trimmings, with red wine to wash it down. Then we went back to George's flat, where he showed me the slides of us all, which were taken during the week I had stayed with Viviane in Jo'burg previously. They were marvellous, especially shown with George's projector on a large screen.

George gave me his spare room for the night and I felt very much at home. Viviane's mother and father, my Aunty Connie and Uncle Eric, had met George when he was in England earlier in the year; and they both liked him very much. He told me to write to my parents, that he was a "confirmed Londoner", in other words he was "as safe as houses"! Or rather I was!

I left Jo'burg early on Monday 2 June and hitched five hundred and fifty miles to Francistown, arriving the next morning, having stayed overnight at a hotel on the way. I had a quiet, restful day at the Roman Catholic Mission, when, again I was given a very warm welcome by the Priests.

Early the next day I flew with the W.N.L.A. aircraft back to the Caprivi Strip in South West Africa; and here I was met by the Rep., Mr Japp who took me to his home, where I stayed with him and his wife for the rest of the day and overnight. By this time I had a heavy cold, my first since arriving in Africa. I had passed through so many different climate zones that it was not surprising! However, Mr and Mrs Japp looked after me very well and managed to get me a lift in a Land Rover the following morning. This enabled me to reach a European couple, who were friends of the Japps; and lived one hundred and ten miles away and forty miles from Senanga.

I stayed overnight with these good people and the next day I travelled twenty-five miles by Land Rover and fifteen by boat, arriving in Senanga at 3pm. The floods had gone down considerably by now; but the road south was still partially covered, hence the boat trip on the Zambezi.

I started work the next day, which was Saturday. Everyone was pleased to see me, particularly the African staff and those on my Ward.

One thing I will always remember was just how clean and tidy my ward had been kept in my absence; and the patients obviously well-cared for. My "boys" had certainly worked conscientiously, even without "sister" presiding over them. This meant I really could trust them to do a good job; I had taught them well and they had proved to be good nurses. I was proud of them!

Chapter Twenty-Three
Back in Senanga

By the time I arrived in Senanga after my trip to South Africa I had covered five thousand and five hundred miles! As I mentioned in a letter to my parents, life here could be lonely at times. However, as the place became increasingly "home" to me these periods were less and less. I really had "fallen in love" with Africa by the time my first year came to an end. I could identify with David Livingstone (a hero of mine!) who had his heart buried in Africa, where he said it truly belonged.

When I arrived back on 6 June 1969, the rains had ceased, the roads had become navigable and the dry season had started. I began to feel the cold! The weather was really the equivalent of a good English summer, the temperature being between 70 and 75 degrees Fahrenheit. It felt cold in the early morning, when it would be about 65 degrees and during the night it was even colder. It really was quite pleasant, I slept better and I now needed two blankets instead of none. I had to write to my mother to send me a couple of knitted, woollen jumpers to wear on the wards in the early morning and at home in the evening. My uniform consisted of a thin white cotton dress, which I wore with sandals; and there was no central heating! I had brought with me two thin cardigans and these were no longer warm enough.

It was great to be back at work again and I was so warmly welcomed both by the staff and patients. I really did feel this was where I belonged. A few days later, Father Lawrence, the Roman Catholic Priest invited us all to a party at his house. There was always a good mix of people, the expatriates from the school and the Hospital, as well as a good number of Zambians who could speak English and were used to mixing socially with Westerners. However, as much fun as these parties were, I still preferred to visit the local people in the villages and dance to the African drums.

This party was to be in fancy dress and I chose to go as a Lozi woman in traditional dress, made especially for me by a local tailor and then finished off by Anna and Pumulo from the Hospital. They even came over to help me on with it and, amidst shrieks of laughter; they told me how to walk and insisted that I danced to one of my African records in it!

On the night of the party they came again to dress me; and I put some brown boot polish on my face. Otherwise without it I looked like a Spanish Gypsy!

It was good to be free to mix with Africans again having only been able to associate with "whites" whilst in South Africa. As I wrote to my brother, in July 1969, I had been happy to be back in "civilisation" once more after nearly a year in the Zambian bush. However, I had missed the simplicity of African life and the peace of the bush. It was strange not to experience this in South Africa, a country predominated by Africans. Yet it was almost completely European in its culture. I wouldn't have wanted to live there, despite it being a rich country with plenty to offer. South Africa didn't have the same culture as in Europe, it being a relatively "young" country, whereas in Senanga I enjoyed authentic African culture, if not the amenities of South Africa.

The only problem I had to face, particularly as a young, single person, was loneliness which could be depressing at times. My Christian faith certainly helped me overcome this and the work I did was very fulfilling. In fact, I never did experience such entire "job satisfaction" either before or since!

When I returned from my epic trip to South Africa I had over forty letters awaiting me! And just as I finished replying to them all, some more arrived! I really needed to write at least one a day in order to keep up. From that time on, I did just that. I appreciated very much so many of my friends and family members wanting to keep in touch with me. But it was hard work sometimes to convey the nature of my work and experience of living in Senanga to the folk back home in England.

Maybe this challenge prepared me for writing this book, something I couldn't have envisaged so many years ago!

Chapter Twenty-Four
Our Orphans

Sometime in early July 1969, we received a grant of five hundred pounds to be able to build an orphanage for our motherless infants. At the time there were thirteen children in one small room; so more space was needed to give them the adequate care they deserved.

Parcels of small knitted vests arrived regularly from my young sister's school. As mentioned in an earlier chapter, Stella's schoolteacher, Miss Steele, a member of the Mothers' Union at the local Parish Church of St. Matthew, organised all this. It must have made my seven-year-old sister very proud to bring home these parcels for my mother to post to me.

I arranged to take some coloured slides of the orphans as well as the small boys on my ward, together with the Male Nurses; and these I sent to the school. The staff and patients were delighted to co-operate in this way and loved having their photos taken.

I know they were well-received at Ashford (Middlesex) Church of England Primary School.

Chapter Twenty-Five
On Safari

In early August I went on a few days' safari. I had a wonderful weekend and was accompanied by my two friends, Angela and Brian who were teachers from the Secondary School. Angela taught English and was from Belfast; Brian came from the Wirral in Cheshire and he taught mathematics. We were very firm friends and we enjoyed the experience in the African Bush immensely.

It was a gentleman, a Scotsman by the name of John Brooks, who lived about forty miles from Senanga, who took us out onto the plain, one hundred miles away.

"Jock" as he was known by his friends, was a Tsetse Fly Control Officer. I had met him when I stayed overnight on the last leg of my journey back to Senanga from South Africa. It was then that he had invited me to go on safari and bring a couple of friends along as well. This was very kind indeed and a most generous offer. It was an opportunity of a lifetime and one not to be missed!

We left one Friday afternoon and returned on the Sunday evening, absolutely "black" – a mixture of both dirt and suntan! We camped out each night. However, although Angela and I had a tent, on the second night I slept outside, as it wasn't too cold. It was wonderful to see the African night sky, so black and clear with myriads of twinkling stars.

There were many wild animals to be seen all in their native habitat. We saw giraffe, three kinds of antelope, wildebeest, wild pigs, guinea fowl and monkeys. There was plenty of elephant spore to be seen, but no elephant, as they were deep into the forest, where it was difficult to drive the Land Rover. At night we could hear the roaring of the lions. They were very near, but not seen, which was just as well!

Jock shot two wildebeest and an antelope and we had quite a feast on the Saturday night. Of course we brought plenty back with us and all the men who worked for Jock (about two hundred in number) were given their fair share.

Angela and I had wildebeest skin each to take back with us as souvenirs. Angela was also given an antelope skin; but I had no need of one as Jock had already given me two, one of which I sent to my parents.

An experience I will never forget was my "bath" in an oil drum! I think it must have been the best I have ever had yet. Jock had an oil drum which had been sawn in half to make it possible to climb into. This was then placed securely on an open fire and the water heated up. It was magnificent!

Chapter Twenty-Six
Warfare

As I wrote home in August 1969, there was trouble in Northern Ireland and I commented on it being more of political conflict than one of religious differences, which I concluded was given as an "age-old excuse". Such were my views then and, indeed, they haven't changed.

We were far removed from such conflict in Zambia although, close to our borders, there was warfare in South West Africa and Angola. This came to our notice when the African freedom fighters came to our hospital for treatment and mothers with young children, who were starving and suffering from malnutrition, arrived in order to escape further deprivation.

Most of the men had received bullet wounds; and they were admitted onto my ward to have these removed and for rest until their wounds had healed.

One little boy, aged nine, was admitted with his father, having had half his face blown off by a land mine. Careful nursing plus daily dressings and antibiotics, prevented infection and saved this lad's life. He lost the sight of one eye and there was a lot of scarring; but, otherwise he made a good recovery. On discharge we referred him to Lusaka for plastic surgery.

Zambia offered political asylum to these people and we were able to help them. One day they were freed from their oppression and we can thank God for that.

Chapter Twenty-Seven
Work at the Hospital Continues

In September 1969, Pierre, the Doctor with whom I had worked for over a year left us to return to France. He had completed his military service and was now free to go home.

We were now awaiting another young doctor to take Pierre's place and, in the meantime, we were very short staffed. Annette was now the only doctor and just Sister Elizabeth and I remained as the only qualified Nurses. Liz had left us temporarily to relieve another missionary Sister for six weeks while she took leave.

Thus, we were very busy. Elizabeth and I were on call twenty-four hours on alternate weeks and Annette was on call all the time. However, I offered to cover for Annette and to call her only when necessary. A lot of the time, an experienced, qualified nurse could cope with most of the medical "emergencies" e.g. malaria, snakebites, burns, etc.

It would be cases such as emergency Caesarean sections or strangulated hernias, when immediate surgery was required, for Annette to intervene. And I was well able to know when to refer such cases to her.

During this time I set up an Antenatal Clinic and a Child Health Clinic, each to be held weekly at our Hospital.

These became very successful. I had many expectant mothers attending, which meant they could be monitored throughout their pregnancy and we would be aware of any forthcoming problems, especially when they were ready to give birth.

I was also able to give my antenatal mothers a mini-lecture at the end of each clinic, entitled "the needs of a pregnant woman". Often their husbands would be waiting outside and listening attentively!

When I emphasised the need for these women to rest during the day, particularly during the later stages of their pregnancy, the menfolk would comment that I was teaching their wives to be lazy! However, this was said with tongue-in-cheek and, although many of these ideas were new to them, I knew they respected my expertise.

It was at this time that I had learned enough of Silozi (the language of the Lozi people) to be able to run the Ante Natal Clinic. This was a great asset, especially when dealing with so many of the village women who had never attended school and whose English was extremely limited. Of course, when absolutely necessary, Kayeye, from my ward, would come to my aid and translate for me.

Chapter Twenty-Eight
Guides

During my leisure time I continued with my Guides, who had just returned to School after the holidays. It was good to see them again and they were all keen to learn which was very encouraging.

My mother had sent me my Guide badge, which "polished up very nicely" after ten years since I'd last worn it! I also made myself a uniform consisting of a light blue cotton dress; and I wore a dark blue neckerchief with an ivory toggle. I was quite pleased with the overall effect and now looked like a proper guide Captain! The girls wore their school uniforms of light blue blouses and maroon skirts and looked very smart.

At our first meeting of term, we elected two Patrol Leaders, whom I'd officially enrolled as Girl Guides the previous term. We subsequently formed two Patrols, one called "Sunflower" and the other "Zinnia". These were two flowers which grew in abundance in Barotse Province and chosen by the Guides themselves.

I also acquired an invaluable assistant who became our "Lieutenant". Her name was Fabia who came from Tanzania and was married to Kumalo, a Zulu from South Africa. They were both Teachers at the Secondary School.

It was a great privilege to get to know Fabia and we became good friends. She had a deep understanding of the girls' background, coming from a rural village herself. Fabia was very well educated and, therefore, an excellent role model for my African Guides. She was the first African girl from Tanzania to have attended University! At the same time she was humble and unassuming, carrying herself with a natural dignity and pride. We made a good team.

It was shortly after Fabia joined us that we took the Guides on their first camping trip. Fabia also brought her two small children, a boy named Kumalo (after his father) aged four and a half; and a girl of eighteen months, called Victoria (named after the famous Lake, in Tanzania, Fabia's mother country). It was lovely to have them with us and the Guides made a huge fuss of them; and so did I!

When it was time for us to leave none of us wanted to go, such a good time we had had together. Both Fabia and I would have loved to stay; but we had to go back to work and the girls to School. However, we returned, really looking forward to going again in the near future.

I really did enjoy running the Guide Company and, certainly having Fabia to help me made a big difference.

Chapter Twenty-Nine
A Letter from Simasiku

In September 1969, I received a parcel of comics which my mother had sent on behalf of my seven-year-old sister, Stella. These were for the small boys on my Ward.

As I have already mentioned, children under five were admitted onto the Children's Ward with their mothers. Therefore, older boys would be admitted to my Ward. In exceptional cases, boys under five years old would have their fathers with them. This was usually because either their mother had died or she had very young children to care for.

One of "my" boys, namely Simasiku, who was admitted with a broken leg, wrote the following "thank you" letter to my sister. It was written in Silozi but here is the English translation:

"Dear young sister of Bo Missy,
I thank you very much for the comics you sent us. I would like to ask you to marry me when you grow up.
I hope this letter will reach you safely.
I am in Grade 2. Which class are you in?
From
Simasiku."

Simasiku returned to the Hospital at Christmas for a check-up in outpatients; and I was able to give him a letter of reply from Stella.

I don't know to this day whether or not she accepted his proposal!

Chapter Thirty
An Error of Judgement

Our day-to-day diet in Senanga could be quite monotonous and it was hard to ring the changes when there was such a lack of variety of foodstuffs. However, I did my best and this experience has stood me in good stead till the present day, as I still nearly always cook from raw ingredients and nothing is ever wasted.

The staple diet of the Africans was "mealie meal" – a stodgy dish, which looked like mashed potato, made from maize flour. The maize was dried in the sun and then the women folk would grind it into a large wooden vessel with a huge pestle, also made from wood.

It was then cooked with water in a large black metal pot on an open fire and stirred very well. Then it would be eaten with your fingers together with meat, fish or vegetables. I got to like it very much when I went camping with the Guides. It certainly filled you up and kept you going for several hours!

When I returned to England I bought several bags of mealie-meal, in South Africa, to take home with me. It was a real treat!

However, until I acquired the taste for mealie-meal (known as "buhobe" in Silozi) and learned how to cook it, I ate mainly rice each day, as did most of the expatriates. Potatoes were very hard to come by; when they occasionally did, they were a real delicacy.

My houseboy used to cook my breakfast before I went to work. This consisted of toast with jam and coffee. At midday he would have my dinner ready for when I finished my morning shift. Whilst on-duty I would "pop" across to the house I shared with Annette and give Taulo (my houseboy) instructions for the meal he was to prepare.

One day I asked him to mash some overripe bananas with some drinking chocolate powder for me to have for pudding. For the main course he was asked to include boiled potatoes, which were fresh from our garden that day.

When I arrived, exhausted and hungry, to have my dinner, my houseboy duly brought me in some meat and vegetables and nothing else. So I reminded him to bring the potatoes and, lo and behold, he came in and quietly delivered a brown, stodgy concoction!

I realised, to my horror, that he had boiled my new potatoes and mashed them with "Nesquik"! If I hadn't valued my dish I would have thrown it at him! I was furious!

Later, however, when I told the others we had a good laugh about it. I also wrote and told my parents; and this too lightened my sorrow at the loss of "fresh new spuds"!

Poor Taulo was quite remorseful and I learned, with humility, that "Man does not live by bread alone." (Matthew 4:4)

Chapter Thirty-One
Planning for My Next Holiday

I wrote to my brother, Jeffrey, in mid-October, 1969 and told him of my plan to travel to Tanzania for my next holiday.

There was going to be an International Conference for all the Medical Volunteers working in Zambia to be held at the University in Lusaka in January 1970. This would be similar to the one I attended at the beginning of the year; and it would assist my travel arrangements very well. I would have my transport paid for by the British Council as far as Lusaka then I could continue my journey, northwards through Zambia and into Tanzania.

I would be able to visit the Copper Belt and experience the contrast between this, a very developed part of Zambia, and Barotse Province, which was the most rural and isolated area of the country, with a traditional way of life that had existed for centuries.

Further north still, I would be able to see the hills and mountains which would be a completed change from the very flat country where I lived and worked.

On leaving Zambia, I planned to take a boat up Lake Tanganyika to the northernmost part of Tanzania and then cross, by land, to Mwanza, on Lake Victoria. Here I planned to stay with Susan and her husband, Jud, who were from America and working as Missionaries with the Africa Inland Mission.

Susan had trained as a Nurse in America; then she had travelled to England to train as a Midwife. It was whilst she was doing Part Two of the course that she worked as a Pupil Midwife in Ashford, Middlesex and delivered my sister, Stella, at home, on 11 January 1962.

I was seventeen years old at the time and worked in a monotonous job as a Junior Designer at Staines Linoleum

Factory. As Susan continued to visit my mother and baby sister for the next ten days after her confinement, I couldn't help but see how happy she was in her work. She would often sing as she went about her duties and she was very popular with all the mothers she had delivered in our neighbourhood.

It was at this time that I decided I wanted to become a Nurse and then train as Midwife!

One day Sister Sterry came to see my mother and sister. She was the qualified Midwife supervising Susan as she continued her training on the District. I took this opportunity to talk to her about my ambition and seek her advice. She very kindly encouraged me and suggested that I apply to one of the London non-teaching hospitals where I would get plenty of experience.

Subsequently, not long before my eighteenth birthday, I applied to St. Stephen's in Chelsea; and in January 1963 I started my training to become a State Registered Nurse.

In 1962 Susan had attended the Billy Graham Crusade in Manchester; and she became a Christian. When she returned to America, after qualifying as a Midwife, she went to Bible College where she met her future husband. In the meantime she wrote to my mother regularly as well as the other mothers she had delivered in their homes. She continued to take a keen interest in all "her babies" and loved to hear how they were progressing.

On completing my nursing and midwifery training in 1967, I applied to the Voluntary Service Overseas, was accepted and "sent" to Africa to my delight, as I didn't really want to go anywhere else. I then wrote to Susan, told her how she had inspired me as a young girl and gave her my latest news.

I also shared with her that I too had become a Christian as a second year student nurse. And, now I believed God was guiding me to work in Zambia.

We corresponded regularly from this time; and when I went to Africa, in 1968, Susan invited me to stay with them which, in due course, I did.

After visiting Tanzania, I wanted to see something of Kenya including the coast and Dar-es-Salaam where I had been invited to stay by Fabia's brother.

More about this later on!

Chapter Thirty-Two
Independence Day 1969

On Friday, 24th October, 1969 Zambia celebrated their Fifth Independence Day, having become a Republic in 1964. They were still part of the British Commonwealth, but no longer a Colony. Formerly the country was known as Northern Rhodesia and belonged to the Federation, which included Barotseland Protectorate, Southern Rhodesia and Nyasaland. Barotseland became Barotse Province and part of Zambia, Southern Rhodesia was now called Rhodesia, later to be known as Zimbabwe and Nyasaland was now called Malawi.

I wrote to my parents with a vivid description of all we did over the weekend of festivities. The previous year I had been on duty, thus unable to participate. However, this year I made up for it in style!

I had a half day off on the Friday and headed straight down to the Boma, on my motor bike, as soon as I was able. This was where everything was going on.

In the morning there had been a march past by representatives (thirty children from each) from all the schools in the Senanga District, with the salute taken by the Governor. The National Anthem was sung and there were speeches given by him and our Minister, Reverend Rene Arriege.

Of course, I missed this; but I was very proud of my Guides who were chosen, together with the Scouts, to march from the Secondary School to the Boma. I was told they were all very smart and orderly!

In the afternoon there was the Primary Schools' Sports which was very enjoyable. There was even a Tug-o'-War consisting of women versus men, which I joined in. We ladies won!

Afterwards all the schools took part in a competition of traditional African dancing to compete for the Independence Cup. It was a very spectacular display; and I enjoyed this event very much.

At the end of Friday's celebrations I was invited, with the other women who were in the Tug-o'-War, to receive our prize of 50 ngwe each (5 shillings sterling) from the "Melena Mukwai" (Chief Princess and the eldest daughter of the late "Litunga") otherwise known as the Paramount Chief. According to protocol we greeted her in the traditional Lozi fashion, crouching low and clapping our hands softly. This was the equivalent of curtseying to our Queen. It was a wonderful experience for me, being the only white person and I felt very honoured!

The weekend was also celebrated to mark the 10th Anniversary of UNIP (United National Independence Party) which governed Zambia.

On Saturday afternoon there was a swimming gala for the Secondary School boys, followed by a canoe race across the River Zambezi, in which I took part.

I entered this with one of my Dressers from the Male Ward, Siyumba and his young brother, Muyunda. We had even paddled our canoe all the way from the Hospital, three miles along the Lagoon which entered the main River Zambezi at the Boma, which was the Civic Centre of Senanga.

Our canoe was made in the traditional African style, dug out from a large tree trunk. It was very long and quite heavy, needing considerable skill to manoeuvre and navigate. In an earlier chapter I described how I learned to paddle one of these. It was great fun!

We came second in the race. However, there was only one other canoe, which was a lightweight kayak, paddled by two of the Russian Secondary School teachers with a small African boy on top, in the middle! In a way we felt that they had cheated; but they had complied with the rules which dictated three people on board. And it was all in good fun, after all.

Siyumbwa, Muyunda and I won 1Kwacha (10 shillings Sterling) each as a prize for our effort for which we were very pleased. Everyone really enjoyed watching this race. They thought I was extremely brave as a woman to cross the Zambezi in such a manner and very clever as a "Mukuwa" (literally translated: "white man") to be able to do it!

On Sunday there were more sports and some traditional dancing. During one of them I was "dragged" out by the District Secretary to join in, accompanied by the beating of African drums! Again, the crowd were delighted and I got a special mention on the loud speaker! I was a bit embarrassed, but, nevertheless, I thoroughly enjoyed myself, wiggling my bottom with them all!

The Zambians were much less inhibited than the average European; so I felt very much at home with them!

In the afternoon, the Mulena Mukwai, District Governor and several of the village Chiefs visited our Hospital. The patients were delighted as well as all the staff on duty. Later these "dignitaries" had tea with us at the Doctor's house. This too was a very special occasion.

The Mulena Mukwai was a very charming woman of about sixty years, a devout Christian and a good friend of Annette. It was a great pleasure and privilege to meet her and I don't think she will ever forget me either!

Chapter Thirty-Three
Life in General

In November 1969 I wrote to my parents, giving them a general account of my current life in Senanga.

Our transport system had been "updated" quite recently inasmuch as the four seater Beavers, flying from Mongu, the capital of Barotse Province, to Senanga, had been stopped. This was a great pity really, because it was a very exciting experience to fly in one of these small aircrafts; and, on the few occasions that I had the opportunity to do so, I thoroughly enjoyed myself.

However, the thirty-two seater Dakota had now replaced the Beaver and flew to Senanga via Livingstone. This meant our transport was now more efficient, or so it would seem.

Before I would receive a letter from my parents each week whereas now they took two or even more to arrive! The main advantage was that the Dakota, which came three times a week, connected us to Lusaka and thereby to Europe, with flights there twice weekly

We now had anew Doctor to take Pierre's place. His name was Marc, who arrived on 5th.November with his lovely young wife, Miriam. They both came from the Alsace region of France, close to the German border. I got on with them both straight away. Marc had a strong Christian faith, as did his wife; and they became a great asset to our little community.

Instead of doing Military Service Marc elected to spend a year with the Paris Mission Society, working at our Hospital. He was going to work with me on the Male Ward, T.B. and Leprosy Sections, during normal working hours; and taking turns with Annette, to be on call outside of these. This, of course, was a great relief for Annette who had become extremely tired of late.

Marc insisted that I spoke to him always in English and not French, so I could help him to become more fluent. This was a sensible suggestion really; but it did mean that I had less opportunity to practise French. In fact, by now, my Lozi was considerably better!

My Guide Company was going from strength to strength. Recently, I'd had another enrolment ceremony, in which seven girls were now officially Girl Guides, bringing our number up to fourteen! I was very proud pf them, as they had worked so hard.

All the Guides were preparing for their Form Two Exam at the end of the month. This was very important, as they would only be able to continue with their Secondary education if they were successful.

It has to be remembered that Secondary education was still very new in Zambia, just five years after Independence. For these girls there was not such a great incentive to study and learn, especially for those who came from such a traditional rural background,

They were the first generation of Africans to attend Secondary School and, therefore, had very few, if any role, models. Their idea of achievement was so vastly different from ours in England and, indeed, in the Western world. This would change eventually, as more people became educated.

I just hoped and prayed that being in the Guide movement was a source of inspiration and that Fabia and I could encourage them to do their very best. It would have certainly been a pity if I had to start all over again with my Guides just as we'd all become used to one another and had made such progress.

It was at this time that I wrote to Mrs Woodhouse, my former Guide Captain in Ashford, Middx, and updated her with news of my Guide Company. I knew she would write back with words of encouragement, both for me and my Guides. It was good, too, for her Guides to know something about Guiding in the African Bush.

In my spare time I did plenty of sewing, making my own uniforms as the others wore out. Eventually I became quite a proficient seamstress, something I never thought possible.

As the saying goes: "Necessity is the Mother of Invention." It certainly was!

Chapter Thirty-Four
My Birthday

On 9th. December 1969 I was twenty-five years old and had been seriously ill. I made light of it when I wrote to my parents, so as not to worry them.

As I write this and look back over the years, I realise just how ill I was. It appeared I had flu and bronchitis, which, at the time, was striking many of our local population, causing several deaths. Those who came on my ward had pneumonia as a complication of flu. Fortunately, more survived than died; but, by the time I had nursed them back to health, I became ill myself.

In a very short time my temperature rose from 101°F to 103°F where it remained as such for two days. I probably had contracted pneumonia; but due to our very basic X-ray machine and the fact that I was too ill to go over to the Hospital, it wasn't officially diagnosed.

Annette, who very rarely showed her emotions, was visibly worried as she took my temperature one morning and it still hadn't dropped. She consequently doubled my intramuscular injections of Penicillin from once to twice daily. I dreaded these and suffered a very sore bottom for days!

The day before my birthday, Jeanette, the School Matron, together with Nicole, the Minister's wife and their children, came to see me. I remember to this day how concerned they both were, in particular Jeannette, herself a qualified nurse. She urged me to drink more. I had tried my best, but found it very hard, being almost too weak to hold a glass and having no appetite

Jeanette, being a good Nurse, immediately poured me a drink and gave it to me. I duly co-operated and drank the whole glass. Thereafter, I began to take fluids at regular intervals and was soon on the road to recovery.

It was during their visit that I was given some unexpected birthday presents: Yardley's talcum powder (much appreciated!) and some "Dairy Box" chocolates which, a lot later on, I really enjoyed. They were very kind and cheered me up no end.

Later on, the same day, Rene the Minister came to see me. His wife, Nicole, must have expressed her concern. The good Pastor, without further delay, took my hand and prayed fervently for the Lord to heal me and restore me to health. Almost straightaway I felt a deep sense of peace; and, knowing I was safe in God's hands, I had no fear.

Miraculously, the next morning, on my birthday, my temperature started to drop. I sweated profusely and literally soaked my bed sheets. Marc's wife, Miriam, came and changed my bed, while I sat in a chair. And, shortly after, Liz gave me a bed-bath. I was so very grateful to them both and, indeed to the Lord for signs of His healing!

Earlier on Annette had "attacked" me with yet another syringe full of Penicillin. I used to dread these injections; and now whenever I had to give one myself I was very sympathetic!

However, the caring Doctor allowed me to get up in the afternoon for a short time; and this really did cheer me up. I still felt very weak but this did me no end of good psychologically. To my great surprise, just as I entered my living room I was greeted by Annette, Elizabeth, Liz and Marc and Miriam, singing "Happy Birthday!" I was being given a party, which I knew nothing about!

Annette had made a cake with six candles on top – a large one denoting twenty years and five small ones. We ate this with cups of freshly brewed tea and I actually enjoyed it. My appetite was returning!

I was even given some more birthday presents – one was a book on Medical Care in the Tropics and the other a toy poodle! I was very pleased with them both, the latter becoming my bed companion as I recuperated!

I was in bed for six days and then I rested for another day before returning to work. I had received Penicillin throughout this time; and it was a great relief to be better and not to have it anymore!

I did feel very weak for several days; and then gradually I began to gain strength as I started to eat more normally again.

I did then and still do praise God for His healing and restoring me; so I could continue to serve Him once more and for many years ahead.

At twenty-five my life was just beginning!

Chapter Thirty-Five
Christmas at the Hospital

It was Christmas once again and my second celebration of this great Feast in Senanga, We were very busy indeed over the Festive season, not so much with medical work (it was quiet for a change!) but with making it a good Christmas for both the patients and staff.

It was so enjoyable that the time simply flew by. Such is always the case! On Christmas Eve we all went round the hospital carol singing (in the language of the Lozi, of course), with homemade lanterns. Earlier that day we had decorated the hospital and it looked quite splendid.

After singing the expatriate staff gathered at Annette's, where we listened to part of Handel's Messiah by candle light. We then heard a Cantata of the Nativity, in French, in which Annette's brother, a Church Minister, was the speaker. It was all both enjoyable, as well as inspiring. Afterwards we had Christmas cake and coffee together before retiring to our beds for a well-earned sleep.

However, mine was delayed as I was on-call for all Maternity cases; and I delivered a baby girl at 11:55 pm! It was well worth it though, and both mother and baby did very well.

We were all up 6:30 am for a prayer and Bible reading on each ward. After, we all went for breakfast, returning on duty at 7.30am.

The orphans were all dressed up in their best clothes and were given their Christmas presents at 8:30 am. Many of these had been sent from the Paris Mission Society in France and Switzerland. I had also received a parcel containing babies' knitted vests and children's clothes, from St. Matthew's Mothers' Union and my mother. I had been able to give these to Sister Elizabeth in time for Christmas.

The children were delighted with the toys they received and I took several photos. These I will always treasure. Their little faces shone with joy. It was a lovely sight to behold.

At 10:00 am, we had our Christmas Day Service outside, under the flamboyant tree at the centre of the hospital. All my patients attended, with the exception of two who were bedridden and too ill to be moved. Even so, a good many of these men had to be carried out by my staff. We had no wheelchairs and the ground consisted of grass and soft sand anyway.

It gave me great pleasure to see these men willingly come along to worship the Lord on such a special occasion. Normally, on a Sunday, it was mainly the female patients who came to Church.

Handel's Hallelujah Chorus was played while everybody made their way to gather together. It was a very beautiful occasion.

After the service we gave all the patients on the Children's Ward their presents. There was condensed milk, oranges, biscuits and sweets for each child with which they and their mothers were very pleased.

I had a little nine-year-old boy on my ward to whom I gave a big highwayman patrol car and his eyes nearly popped out of his head! He was absolutely thrilled to bits!

By this time we were ready for dinner; so we all went to our separate homes for a simple meal and a short rest. We then returned to the hospital at 2:30 pm in time for our Christmas party. This was attended by the children of all our staff. Together with their parents we had at least one hundred people! Needless to say, it was enjoyed very much by us all.

Fortunately, it was still very quiet at the hospital with no emergencies arising. There were just the routine tasks to be done; so we had the time to celebrate Christmas together in style!

At 5:00 pm we had a party in our garden for us expatriates and all our staff, including our houseboys and their families. They were all given Christmas presents – cigarettes for the men and tins of condensed milk for their wives. The female hospital staff were also given books on sewing, cooking and laundry work. All of them appreciated these gifts very much, which were real treats and things they would never buy. The girls, who were mainly the Nurses and able to read English, were delighted with their books.

In the evening we had our own party for all the Mission staff, from the Hospital and the Mission Stations in Senanga, Sefula and Mongu. There were about twenty-five of us, including the children. We also had our present-giving; and we were as delighted as any of the children to receive them.

By now we were all too tired to be very lively, as can be imagined. Nevertheless, we enjoyed ourselves eating, talking and singing a few carols in both French and English. We then all retired to our beds at around midnight and slept like "logs".

It had been a good day!

Chapter Thirty-Six

"Inasmuch as ye did it unto one of the least of these my brethren, ye have done it unto me"
Matthew 25:40

On Boxing Day I cooked a duck with orange sauce. My houseboy, Taulo, had fetched it from nearby Litambya village and had made an excellent job of cleaning it. This would be my first time to cook this dish, known in French as "Canard a l' orange". As I had invited Annette, Elizabeth and a young lady by the name of Denise, all of whom were French I was somewhat apprehensive!

Liz, who was Dutch, also came and they all told me that it was delicious! Indeed, it was; and I was very pleased with what I had done. More importantly, we had all enjoyed the meal together as well as each other's company.

Incidentally, Denise was a friend of Rene and Nicole; and staying with them at the Mission Station for the Christmas holiday.

After our "feast", Annette took Denise and me in the Land Rover to Likulwe, two miles along a sandy track from our hospital. This was our Leprosy Settlement. Here the victims of this cruel disease lived, with their families, as normal a life as was possible.

Likulwe was built as a traditional rural African village and all its residents lived as any other African in the Zambian Bush. However, the one exception was that a Medical Orderly lived there too, together with his family. These meant that those with Leprosy could be monitored carefully and receive their medication and any other necessary treatment.

Leprosy is not as contagious as many might think. It is usually prolonged, intimate contact over many years during which the disease can be transmitted. Of course, poor living conditions, such as they were in the rural areas, increased the risk of contracting the illness.

The main problem facing a person with Leprosy is the damage to the nerves and, therefore a lack of feeling, especially in the hands and feet; thus, the risk of losing fingers and toes when injury, which cannot be felt, occurs. Fire burns and handling hot cooking utensils presented a big risk, as did walking barefoot.

The Leprosy patient had to be educated to use footwear (sandals made from old tyres were ideal and very economical!); and to protect their hands when cooking over an open fire, or wielding an axe to chop wood, for example.

Many needed clean dressings, applied daily, to open sores to prevent infection arising. This task was carried out by the Medical Orderly. Should the health of any deteriorate, they would come to our Hospital for further treatment. Annette, our Doctor, used to visit regularly, so she could bring any patient back with her, if necessary and generally oversee the settlement.

As it was Christmas, our visit was a special one. We took with us presents for all the men and women in Likulwe. There were shirts and shorts for the menfolk; and for the women cotton blouses and "wrap-round" African print cloths (similar to a sarong and known as a "mulepo" in Lozi). They were, needless to say, very grateful for these gifts; and it was a joy to see them all so pleased.

We also had a short service of prayers, hymns and a Bible reading, which Annette conducted. We all joined in this joyful occasion of celebration of our Saviour's birth and were very blessed.

I think I can honestly say, I had never spent a better Christmas. It had been so enjoyable throughout and this visit to the Likulwe Leprosy Settlement was truly the "icing on the cake".

To this day I cannot forget what a blessing it had been for me.

Later on Boxing Day, we gave a small party for all the girls working at the Hospital. Most of these were the Nurses, including our two Maternity Assistants, Anna and Pumulo and the rest being the staff from the orphanage. Most of the Male

Nurses were married with their own families with whom they could celebrate Christmas, whereas the girls were on their own.

It was very enjoyable for all of us, including Annette, Liz, Elizabeth and myself, who were also present. We enjoyed some lovely food together, consisting of various salads, homemade bread and cakes, with tea and fruit juice to drink.

Elizabeth and Liz had worked hard preparing the salads whilst Annette and 1 were at Likulwe. Our houseboys made the bread; and somehow Annette and I had managed to make the cakes in our "spare" moment!

We all sang some Lozi Christmas hymns and generally had a good time celebrating this wonderful Feast together. It had, indeed, been one of the best Christmases I had ever had and certainly one I have never forgotten.

Chapter Thirty-Seven
Thank You!

The next day, in the evening, I gave a small tea party for the Harrington children, who were all home for the Christmas holidays. There were ten of us present, including myself and two cousins.

Willie and Dinah Harrington were a well-to-do "coloured" (i.e. Euro-African) family living nearby. Willie owned a bar in Senanga, which on one occasion I visited in the evening. William, who by that time had finished at college; and was working for his father was there; so I felt quite comfortable in what was a very male domain.

It was a very interesting experience and I was made most welcome. The men, most of whom were married, were dancing together to the sound of Jim Reeves, who was then extremely popular with the Africans, coming from the jukebox! They were obviously enjoying themselves; and almost abstemious where alcohol consumption was concerned.

Mr and Mrs Harrington had five sons and one daughter, Peggy aged ten. All but one son, Michael, lived away from home, either in Livingstone or Lusaka. The eldest son, Jimmy, was at university and the other children were at school or College.

Michael suffered from Epilepsy and had been brain damaged since birth. He was a regular visitor to our Hospital as an outpatient; with daily medication his fits were under control and he kept well. His mother, Dinah, was a lovely lady and she would always drive him to us in her Land Rover. It was always a pleasure to see her and we were all very fond of Michael.

Both Willie and Dinah had been very good to me ever since my arrival in Senanga. Indeed, it was Ann, my predecessor, who had introduced me to the Harrington family before she returned to England. Since then I had always been welcomed in their home and made to feel one of the family.

The little party I gave was a good way to say "Thank You!"

Chapter Thirty-Eight
The Medical Conference

Early in January 1970, I set off to Lusaka, by plane via Livingstone, to attend a Medical Conference at the University of Zambia. This was for all medical volunteers working in Zambia; and it lasted for four days.

I spent a week altogether in Lusaka, staying with the Burgess family for a few days, both before and after the conference, and at the University in the Students' accommodation for its duration.

Whilst staying with the Burgess family, Mrs B. had to go into Hospital for an emergency Cholecystectomy (removal of the gall bladder); and for the first two nights post operatively I nursed her, for which Mr Burgess was very grateful. The Hospital was very short-staffed; so they were both reassured by my being there. It was the least I could do as they had been so kind to me when I first arrived in Zambia.

It was quite a change nursing in such a modern hospital after our humble hospital in the African Bush! Although I was very tired I valued the experience.

The Medical Conference was extremely interesting and I enjoyed it very much. It was good to meet the other volunteers and, in particular, Jo, a nurse from England and, like myself, also working in a Bush Mission hospital, in another part of Zambia. Jo and I had already met at our VSO briefing courses in London and Edinburgh before coming to Zambia; and we had become good friends. We had kept in touch and wrote regularly to each other.

At the Conference, several notable doctors were present and gave us lectures each day; some were employed by the Government and others were Missionary Doctors, working in the

African Bush. Between them they had a vast amount of experience; and we were given plenty of "food" for thought.

The main topic was "Maternity and Child Care in Developing Countries:" and present at our lectures were the students from the University's School of Medicine. These would be Zambia's first "home-grown" Doctors. It was good to be able to meet these young men and I encouraged them to remain in Zambia to be able to help their own people, especially in the rural areas. They did express interest; and I sincerely hope they heeded my advice!

Not only did the Conference provide much mental stimulation; but we also had an excellent social life whilst there! Something was planned for us each evening.

The first evening there was a party given by one of the doctors. Then, the following day, there was a cocktail party (very "posh"!) at the British High Commissioner's home for the British Volunteer.

On Saturday evening there was a dance at the University for all the participants of the Conference plus the Students, which was great fun. On Sunday we were invited to a sumptuous barbeque at the Dutch Volunteers' Centre in Lusaka; and Monday evening all us "second year" VSO's went out for the evening and "painted the town red"!

It made such a very pleasant change after the bush life. Furthermore, we were able to relax and enjoy ourselves after the hard work we had all been doing. It was very much appreciated by one and all.

I was now in a holiday mood and prepared for my next adventure!

Chapter Thirty-Nine
My Trip to East Africa

Part One: Northern Zambia

I left Lusaka in mid-January having obtained a lift with one of the Doctors and two Dutch Nurses with whom I had attended the Medical Conference. We travelled together, via the Copper Belt, to Manza, in the Northern Province, where we stayed overnight

It was an interesting experience to see the Copper Belt, which is the most developed part of Zambia, with a more Westernised lifestyle than most of the rest of Zambia, including Barotse Province. Certainly there were plenty of opportunities here for qualified nurses from Britain and very good pay besides! However, I wouldn't have swapped my life in Senanga and the work I did there for a job in any of the Copper Belt Hospitals, however highly paid I would have been.

From Manza, I had a lift to Kasama with the Provincial Officer of Police (a Zambian) where I stayed overnight with a Church of Scotland Missionary, who I had met in Edinburgh on the VSO briefing course we had both attended before coming to Zambia. We had kept in touch ever since; and it was good to see each other again and exchange our news.

The next day I had a lift to Abercorn where I spent the weekend with a U.C.Z. (United Church of Zambia) Minister and his wife. They were both English and had been sent by the Congregational Council for World Mission (C.C.W.M.) as it was known then. (Sometime later the Congregational Church amalgamated with the English Presbyterian Church and the United Reformed Church came into being.)

Formerly the C.C.W.M. had been the "London Missionary Society" and it was this organization that had sent Doctor David

Livingstone to the Colony of Northern Rhodesia, as Zambia was then, before Independence.

David Livingstone was an explorer as well as Missionary Doctor; and he had been largely responsible for putting the country well and truly "on the map" including his great discovery of the Victoria Falls and the route of the River Zambezi.

We had studied Livingstone's journeys in our Geography lessons when I was a second year pupil at Grammar School; and this part of Africa had remained a fascination for me ever since. Indeed, David Livingstone was one of my heroes!

Abercorn is the northernmost part of Zambia, close to the border with Tanzania; and the landscape, with its hills and mountains, was so very different to the flat plains of Barotse Province.

There is also a Church (once L.M.S. and now U.C.Z.), built in honour of David Livingstone, now an Ancient Monument yet less than two hundred years old! I found it quite significant that the Christian Gospel, which has permeated our culture in the West over the past two thousand years, has only taken root in the Continent of Africa in very recent years, by comparison. Yet in a relatively short time these "young" countries, such as Zambia, with their Democratic Governments and emphasis on Education and Health Care, have made great progress. These institutions we take so much for granted in England, and we so easily forget that they have their roots in the Christian Gospel.

I enjoyed my time with my new friends and their three young children, at the Mission Station in Abercorn, very much. They felt a bit isolated and somewhat lonely where they were; and they made me very welcome indeed. We were all sorry to say "goodbye" when the time came for me to go; and they assured me of their prayers as I continued my journey to Tanzania.

Part Two: Tanzania
"From Abercon to Mwanza"

I left Abercorn in a lorry in which I was given a lift, for two hundred and twenty-five miles, to Mpala in Tanzania. I spent two nights there "lavished with wonderful hospitality" (as I wrote in a letter to my parents) by the "White Sisters" – a Roman Catholic

Community of Nuns, working as Missionary Nurses and Teachers.

These dear ladies treated me like one of their own, even addressing me as "Sister". I vividly remember an evening when we had a "sing-song" with one of the nuns playing a guitar; this was so enjoyable and spiritually uplifting.

One of the Sisters was a School Teacher, and had taught my friend Fabia, who was now a Lieutenant in our Guide Company, in Senanga. I had mentioned Fabia and she was able to tell me how proud she had been of her and what a privilege to have taught her and prepare her for entry to University – the first Tanzanian African girl to do so.

I left Mpala and then travelled by bus to Mwanza, close to Lake Victoria, where I stayed with Susan and Judd. They have been mentioned already in a previous chapter; and were now house parents to thirteen children aged between six and eleven years old whose parents were Missionaries, working for the African Inland Mission throughout Tanzania.

These children attended the local Mission Primary School and lived with Susan and Judd and their little eighteen-month-old son, Adam. They had a large house on a hillside situated on the banks of Lake Victoria, sixty-five miles from the town of Mwanza. It had a beautiful outlook across the Lake; and as soon as I saw it I made it my intention to have a swim there!

It was good to see Susan again after eight years, when she had delivered my sister, Stella in 1962. Susan too was delighted to see me and introduce me to her husband, Judd. There was never a dull moment in their home with so many children being there and I had a great time during the five days I stayed with Susan and Judd. This included a swim in Lake Victoria; and, despite the risk of contracting Bilharzia (a waterborne parasitic disease) I was safe!

Susan wrote to my parents after I left Mwanza and assured them that I was "fine and really enjoying my trip" and telling them not to worry about me. She expressed how pleased they had been to see me and wished I could have stayed longer. She conveyed her greetings to the whole family and requested my mother to send her some recent photos of Stella.

What a blessing it was for us all to have renewed contact with each other in this way!

Part Three: Kenya
"Mwansa to Mombasa"

From Mwansa I headed for the East Coast of Tanzania, via the Serengeti Game Reserve, to Mombasa, in Kenya

My original plan had been to travel via Mount Kilimanjaro – Africa's highest mountain – to Mombasa. This spectacular mountain could be seen from Mwansa with its snow-capped peak rising majestically into the sky above.

I had hoped to climb to the summit before arriving in Mombasa. However, this required a lot more preparation than I had time for; and in itself was, at least, a five-day trek. I consoled myself with a few days relaxing on the beach and swimming in the sea in the Indian Ocean instead!

Another pertinent reminder was that I had booked a flight from Livingstone to Senanga; and first I had to fly from Lusaka! I was determined to arrive back to work at the Hospital, on time and in one piece!

I travelled from Mwanza, through the Serengeti Game Reserve, to Arusha by bus. Incidentally, public transport was both cheap and reliable in Tanzania and I was able to explore this beautiful country quite easily, at a very low cost.

Going through the Game Reserve was a wonderful experience and certainly one of a lifetime. There I was on a local bus all Africans, except myself and a young Arab schoolboy called Mbarak, experiencing a Safari, without paying an exorbitant cost to do so! I was able to see almost every kind of African wildlife in their natural habitat and the sight of them was truly amazing!

During our journey a group of Massai Tribesmen boarded the bus for a few miles. They were dressed in their traditional clothes which consisted of loincloths and carrying spears! These men were hunters and gatherers, living as they had done for hundreds of years. Their diet was simple, but very nutritious, consisting mainly of goat's blood and milk. And this accounted for the unusual smell which pervaded the bus!

I had encountered many human odours in my time; but never one such as this! I soon got used to it, however; and then I couldn't help but admire the sheer beauty of these men. They were very tall with skin which was light brown and so smooth it looked as if it had been polished; and they bore themselves with dignity and pride.

Mbarak was at Secondary School and aged sixteen. He spoke very good English and was happy to sit with me so he could practise it. In fact we became good friends and kept in touch during the rest of my time in Africa.

He showed a keen interest in my Christian beliefs, as I did his Muslim faith. I used to send him portions of Scripture, written in Arabic, obtained from the Scripture Gift Mission in London, which he was always pleased to receive.

One big impression Mbarak made upon me was his sincere devotion to Allah. During our journey when it was midday he asked me to excuse him while he prayed and then proceeded to bow low and pray quietly. I was very impressed!

We also had an exciting adventure en route. Along the way we came to a river which, owing to a heavy rainfall, had flooded the main road. It was far too deep to traverse by bus; so we waited several hours for the water to abate to a level safe enough to continue.

Every half hour or so some of the men would wade across with wooden stakes testing the depth until we could continue our journey. And the womenfolk, who had their pots and pans with them as well as fresh maize, made a large fire on which they roasted "mealies" sufficient for us all.

Certainly the Lord provided!

At Moshi I was picked up by two young Indian men who were brothers, named Mohammed and Bulsara. They were perfect gentlemen and I couldn't have been in safer hands than I was with these two devout followers of Islam.

I was taken two hundred miles to the beautiful coastal town of Malindi, seventy-five miles from Mombasa, where I spent the weekend of a lifetime.

Mohammed and Bulsara treated me as they would their own sister, and we spent a wonderful time together camping on the beach, beside the Indian Ocean. They shared a tent and I had one to myself!

We swam in the sea many times and in the evenings visited nearly every nightclub and hotel in town – all very "lush" places laid on for the European tourists. One of them was patronised by a host of "mad" Germans and we were able to partake of their barbeque supper on the house!

Another place we went to had tribal dancing laid on; and, at an African club where we ended up on our final night together, there was a fire-eating display! We then went back to our "camp" and had a swim in the sea at 2 o'clock in the morning!

The next day we went to Mombasa and I was treated to a "real" Indian meal. It was there that I learned to eat rice, with my fingers, in the correct Indian style. I was taught well by my new friends all that I needed to know about their etiquette when eating; and I am so grateful to this very day.

We were sad when it was time for us to part company. Mohammed and Bulsara then made their way back to their home in Tanzania, but not before making sure I was "installed" safely at the "Coast School for Physically Handicapped Children" run by two Physiotherapists who were VSO's from England.

They very kindly allowed me to stay with them for two nights, before I travelled back to Tanzania. This enabled me to see something of Mombasa, a very old port, which I found fascinating and quite cosmopolitan, with its many Arab sailors.

Part Four: Tanzania Re-Visited
"Dar-es-Salaam"

My good friend, Fabia had written to her brother, Gerald, who was the Chief Commissioner of Police in Dar-es-Salaam, where I had travelled overnight by bus from Mombasa. She had also given me Gerald's address and telephone number; thus I was able to contact him quite easily.

I had a wonderful time with Gerald and his family, consisting of his wife and five sons. I was given marvellous hospitality; and, during the few days I spent with them, I was taken sightseeing all over the city. I was told that as I was a friend of their sister, Fabia, I was also, according to their African customs, their sister too; and I was certainly treated as such!

Indeed, Gerald, who was the eldest in his family, wrote a lovely letter to my parents telling them of my visit and how delighted they had been to meet me. He also told them, that according to their "tribal African traditions" my parents were also relatives! (I still have this letter, written in perfect English in beautiful "script" handwriting). Oh, how much I treasure these heartfelt concepts!

During my stay I was given mainly traditional East African food, the exception being rice instead of their staple diet of "mealie meal" – a thick mix of ground maize and water. This would be eaten with your fingers as opposed to rice for which I was given a spoon! When I told Gerald that I had eaten mealie-meal on many occasions with my African friends in Senanga it was on the table for every meal we shared together afterwards; and the whole family were delighted!

It was shortly after this that I was taken on a family picnic at a nearby beach. Here we all sat under a palm tree eating and drinking homemade palm wine. It was one of the highlights of my visit to this lovely family and something I will never forget.

In 1970, when I visited Tanzania, the country had not been independent for long. President Nyerere was its first African president once it ceased to be a British Colony. Gerald was one of several Africans who, although having only completed Primary School, took over from the British Civil Servants. They were to be admired for their loyalty and dedication to this new country, its people and their President.

"Dar es Salaam to Zambia"

I hitchhiked all the way from Dar-es-Salaam, via the border with Zambia, to Lusaka. Most of my lifts were with the big lorries of which there was a steady stream from Dar-es-Salaam, our nearest port, to Zambia.

The exception was a lift I was given by the African Manager of the Tanzanian Tourist Corporation and his staff

The aforesaid Manager kindly arranged for me to be accommodated and entertained in one of their hotels, en route to the Zambian border, for which I was very grateful. I remember being quite tired by then, having travelled such a long way that day; so I really did appreciate the comfort I was provided. Yet another occasion to thank God for his provision!

My journey from Dar-es-Salaam to the Zambia Border took me through the towns of Iringa and Mmbeya, all situated along the main "trunk" road, albeit dirt track to Lusaka.

So far I was safe and sound, with just a few hundred miles to go in order to meet my friends, Mr and Mrs Burgess before flying to Livingstone.

Certainly I had met some wonderful people during my time in East Africa and had experienced hospitality from people of all the main ethnic groups living there, African, Asian and European. This was, indeed something I would never forget.

Chapter Forty
The Return Journey

A Terrific Ordeal

Having reached the Zambian border, I decided to hasten my journey to Lusaka, by taking a night lorry all the way.

This was a big mistake!

In the early evening, while it was yet daylight, I was picked up by a Somali African lorry driver. His English was limited; but we were able to communicate; and he promised to take me all the way to Lusaka.

The driver was on his own, and would usually continue to drive through the night with a short rest and something to eat on the way. However, my driver decided he was going to have a sleep and, to my horror, he climbed up onto the bunk in the back of the cab, on which I had been sleeping!

Instinctively, as I woke up, I knew something was wrong and I had to keep calm. This man had stripped to his underpants and had a knife in his hand!

His intent was to rape me. He tore at my clothing; but fortunately I was wearing a pair of Levi jeans (very strong!) and a polo neck sweater. These were suitable for travelling at night when it was a lot cooler; and I was determined to keep them on!

However, this infuriated my Somali "friend" and he dropped his knife and proceeded to strangle me! Just as I was "blacking out" he let go and I gasped for breath. Another few seconds and I'd have been a "goner". It didn't bear thinking about!

The ordeal wasn't over yet. The man picked up his knife and held it to my body and I felt the tip of the blade pressing into my flesh.

What could I do now? It was around 2:00 am, on a pitch-black African night, on a deserted road. There was no point in screaming; nobody would hear.

So I called out to the Lord, who has said in His Word, "And call upon me in the day of trouble: I will deliver thee, and thou shalt glorify me." (Psalm 50:15)

I prayed aloud and asked for the protection of the Blood of Christ and, immediately the man let go of me, dropped his knife and started to curse and blaspheme. Instantaneously, I reached to the floor and miraculously recovered my glasses, which had been torn off my face and without which I can hardly see. I picked up my bags, literally threw myself out of the cab and landed on my feet!

Within a few minutes, I saw the headlights of a lorry approaching! I stood in the middle of the road and flagged it down; and in the meantime "my driver" had disappeared out of sight.

The lorry stopped for me, opened the cab door, and I was helped inside. There were two drivers, both from Tanzania. By this time I was hysterical; but I managed to convey that I was travelling to Lusaka.

These two men were the essence of kindness. While one drove the lorry the other made me lie down on the bunk at the back and kept stroking my head, speaking words of comfort in Swahili. I knew I was safe and truly thanked God for His protection and provision.

I was taken safely to Lusaka by these two African gentlemen; and I will be eternally grateful to them both.

"Lusaka to Livingstone"

I stayed with the Burgess family for two days and, as always, they looked after me very well, treating me like one of their own daughters.

The first morning I was there, Mrs Burgess asked me what the red marks on my neck were. (I didn't realise they were there!)

Tearfully, I related my story to her and she asked permission to tell her husband which I did, of course.

Straightaway, Mr Burgess located the address of a lorry haulage company in Lusaka and took me to see the Manager.

It was extremely hard for me to relate what had happened; but I did. I must have been shaking like a leaf, because he offered me a cigarette, for which, at the time, I was very grateful!

The Manager had an idea who the Somali driver was; and he assured me that he would lose his job. This did give me a great sense of justice being done; and for me not to recriminate myself for what had happened.

However, it was a long time, in fact over twenty years, before I could talk about it.

I know that, by God's grace, I have been able to forgive this man from Somalia; and I have been healed from all the repercussions of such a horrific ordeal.

Thank you Lord for your mercy!

"Livingstone to Senanga"

I took a flight from Lusaka to Livingstone, having reluctantly said goodbye to the Burgess family who had been so good to me over the past few days. To my dismay, when I arrived in Livingstone I discovered my flight had been cancelled! After spending a day there with a local Methodist Missionary Society family, I was able to arrange alternative transport.

The Manager of the Zambezi River Transport gave me a free pass all the way to Sesheke, one hundred and thirty-five miles away. This involved travelling in a Land Rover for several miles and then taking a passenger barge, for twenty-four hours, along the River Zambezi.

This was far more exciting, albeit a lengthier journey! It was a great experience, and one I shall never forget.

I then had a lift to Sioma, where I stayed at the Roman Catholic Mission. My one vivid memory was being taken by a young Irish Priest to the Sioma Falls and him encouraging me to write a book about my time in Africa! Forty-seven years later this became a reality!

The pontoon to Senaga was out of action; instead I was taken on a fifty h.p. police boat, all the way!

On arrival at the Boma, in Senanga, I was given a lift to the Hospital in a Police Land Rover. I was now back "home"!

Everyone was really pleased to see me, including the African staff and the Hospital patients. I had sent Annette a telegram to say I was coming on a barge from Livingstone; and she hadn't expected me to arrive as soon as I did!

Chapter Forty-One
Back to Work

On my arrival I received two parcels, one with knitted vests for our baby orphans, another with toys and colouring books for the older children, and some Guide magazines from Mrs Woodhouse and her Guides, all of which were very much appreciated. Shortly after, my young sister, Stella, sent sweets for the children on my ward. Needless to say, they were very pleased!

It was good to be back at work again and I was enjoying it immensely. I had missed everybody while I was away and didn't want to think about going back to England in six months' time. This was very different to how I had felt a year ago, when I was quite homesick.

I truly loved my life in Senanga. I looked forward to seeing all my friends, family and London (in that order!); but I had mixed feelings about returning to the U.K. I had now settled to my life in the African Bush and it had become "home" to me.

The work I did at the Hospital, I found extremely satisfying and fulfilling. I was beginning to see some results of my efforts and labour. I had run a course of lectures, in the theory of Nursing; and Anatomy and Physiology, for the Zambian Male Nurses. I had also set them an exam in which they all did quite well, with Kayeye gaining a Distinction!

I also set up a weekly Antenatal Clinic, as well as a Child Health Clinic for the under-fives; and I hoped they would continue for long after I left. At the time, President Kaunda and his Government were behind this work and were promoting preventive Medicine throughout Zambia, which was very encouraging.

Years later, in 1985, when working as a Lifeguard at Acton Baths in London, I met a man, who was one of our regular customers and had visited Zambia. He told me that he had contracted Malaria whilst there and had been admitted into Senanga Hospital. No longer did any of the expatriates I knew work there. Instead it was run by Dutch Missionaries. My friend said he had been well looked after and had made a good recovery. It was still going strong; and the good work was continuing!

Chapter Forty-Two

"Thy word is a lamp unto my feet and a light unto my path."
(Psalm 119:105)

The verse quoted above was so true! Not only did the Lord guide me each day through life (although I was not always aware of this); but in the dark African nights when I was called out to deliver a baby. At such times I would walk along the sandy track, for about a quarter of a mile, to the Hospital from my home, with only an oil lamp to light my path. The light would be just enough for me to take a step and so I would proceed, with one at a time.

Not only did I need to find my way; but it was essential that I would be able to see any snakes or scorpions en route!

Since returning from my trip to East Africa, I was very busy indeed. Elizabeth had gone to France for three month's leave, which meant me taking charge of the Children's Ward and the Orphanage, as well as being on call for Maternity cases, outside of normal working hours, on alternate weeks. I also continued to be responsible for the Male Ward, T.B. and Leprosy Sections. So my work was truly cut out!

When Elizabeth did return, Liz went to Holland for two months; so I was kept very busy right up until I left Senanga. Nevertheless, despite being very tired, I loved my work and the time went far too quickly.

During March 1970, one of my letters to my parents illustrates very well just how busy I could be. I had only managed to get to bed at 5:00 am, after delivering triplets; and then I was back on duty at 7:30 am!

I delivered so many babies during the two years I was in Zambia that I lost count of the exact number. It was always a thrill to deliver a live baby; and it never ceased to be a moving experience.

However, there were times when it was a sad occasion; for instance, a baby was born stillborn, or so premature its chances of survival were very slim. We didn't have the sophisticated facilities that we had at home, such as incubators, for example. We just had to do the best we could, in the circumstances, with only basic equipment.

Fortunately, such sad occasions were rare; and regular attendance at my Antenatal Clinic helped prevent some of these incidents, by looking after the health of these expectant mothers.

With us being well-qualified as Midwives we were also able to prevent infection; and our mothers could have a safe delivery. Our facilities were equivalent to doing home deliveries in England, yet without access to modern Hospital facilities, if needed, in an emergency.

On the whole, the African women from the local villages had small babies in comparison with women in England. Therefore they didn't experience too much difficulty in pushing their babies out into the world; thus there were less vaginal tears. As a result, I rarely had to perform an episiotomy.

However, occasionally the mother would sustain a tear and it would be my responsibility to stitch her up. In England it would be the Doctor on call who would do this. I had seen so many at home, that I was quite able to do this task. But our beds didn't have a dropped end or lithotomy poles; so I had to improvise.

I used to bring the mother to the foot of the bed, sit on a hard wooden chair and ask her to place her feet on my shoulders. Then, by the light of a hurricane lamp, held by one of the African nurses, I would perform the task required!

Thus, I was guided in more than one way by the light of a lamp!

Chapter Forty-Three
Writing Letters

As this is a book about letters, the title of this chapter is very apt!

Unfortunately, during April 1970 both Annette and I had our fountain pens stolen. Mine was a Parker with an Italic nib, which I had received for my twenty-first birthday. I treasured it, as I always used a fountain pen, ever since learning "real writing" in Primary School.

I now had to resort to a ballpoint pen when writing my numerous letters. Just as I got up to date more would arrive! I loved hearing from folks back home; but I was often too tired to reply; nevertheless, I kept going.

To this day, yes even with the internet and email, I write with pen and ink. Not only does it look better and is more personal, it also helps prevent your handwriting deteriorating, especially at my age!

Honesty was a valued trait among the Lozi. (I could trust my houseboy, Taulo, one hundred per cent.) We knew the fifteen year boy who had stolen our pens; and, in Annette's case, money. He worked at the Hospital as a cleaner.

Annette reported the incident to the Police; but it was very likely the objects had been sold by that time. It certainly was very unusual for this to happen in a traditional rural area, in the bush. Certainly, in some of the urban areas crime was more prevalent, in particular petty theft; but not where we were living.

Indeed, according to the older tribal customs, thieves would have their fingers cut off. Thus, the traditions of honesty still remained a valued trait of the typical Lozi; but not, thank God, the punishment!

Chapter Forty-Four
Guides and Scouts

Our Guide Company continued to flourish and, at the end of each term, over the past year, we met with the Secondary School Scouts for a campfire. By now I had the help of one of the Primary School Teachers, her brother also being a Teacher and a Scout Leader. She was a great help to me now that Fabia was on maternity leave.

The School Scout Troup was led by a "schoolboy", the same age as me, whose name was Mubita. He was in his final year at Secondary School and played the guitar very well – far better than me! I sold Mubita mine, as I was making so little progress and he was thrilled to bits with it.

Our campfires proved to be very popular and most enjoyable. We made cocoa in a large, black iron pot on an open fire and sang songs, some African and others the traditional Guide and Scout campfire songs in English, many of which I taught them.

When these young Zambians sang, they put their heart and soul into it and they injected a very typical African style into their songs. It was a pleasure to hear them and be part of making music in such a novel way.

There were one hundred of us gathered together when the schools broke up for Easter in 1970. Scouts and Guides from the Primary and Secondary Schools joined together; and our newly appointed Commissioner for the Scouts in Barotse Province came along and made everything "go with a swing".

At the beginning of term we'd had a joint service of worship for "Thinking Day" (in honour of our founder, the late Lord Baden-Powell). This was so enjoyable that we that we planned to have another at the beginning of the next term.

Later, during May, encouraged by the success of our "Thinking Day" Service, we had a "Guides' and Scouts' Own". This was an act of Christian worship which was arranged and organised by the Guide and Scout Leaders. We invited our District Secretary to be our speaker, he was delighted to attend and we were all very blessed.

I also planned to take the Guides camping again; and would be enrolling many of my new Form One recruits, which was always a great pleasure.

By now the rains had stopped. In fact, during 1970 we had very little rain and by mid-April the leaves were falling and everything was turning brown. This usually occurred in June; so winter had arrived early. Although it was hot during the day, it was quite cool at night. This was really the best time of the year and sleep became more refreshing once again.

Chapter Forty-Five
Our New Children's Home

On the 5 May 1970, we had the cornerstone laying ceremony for our new "Motherless Infants' Home," otherwise to be called the "Children's Home". This was, indeed, a big event at our Hospital.

First we all sang the Zambian National Anthem, then our Doctor gave her address. This was most interesting, as Annette had worked in Senanga since 1948 and had designed and supervised the building of the "Paris Mission Society Senanga Hospital", as it was then named.

In 1952 Dr Annette Casalis had written, at the end of her report on P.M.S. Medical Work, "When this Hospital will be open, it should be completed by a Nursery as soon as possible." Eighteen years later her wish was accomplished. Annette was more than satisfied.

During 1948 she delivered her first baby, who was now (in 1970) the mother of two "big boys". Since then there were so many babies who were left motherless, the Mission Chairman had advised closing this section of the work "for financial reasons and for the health of the staff", who were already over-worked.

For a period of six years the only motherless infants admitted were accompanied by a relative, for which there was very little room.

In 1958 the nursery was re-opened, as there was now an extra Doctor and Sister to supervise the work.

Many children slept on mats; and as soon as any of the few beds were empty, a new child was admitted! Most of these were under the care of one member of staff; and, whereas between 1952 and 1957 there were only two admissions, the total up-to-date was now eighty-five.

In previous times when a mother died in childbirth, her baby would be buried with her! This was possibly to save there being two funerals, as the child would not survive without its mother's milk.

Bottle-feeding in the rural areas, with lack of knowledge and suitable facilities for sterilisation, would present a problem. The risk of Gastroenteritis in such young infants was great.

The ideal, therefore, was to be able to admit the child with a family member. However, this too presented a problem, as the relative would need to stay in the Hospital for at least a year, until the child was weaned.

The intermediate solution, which was in practice when I arrived in Senanga, was to employ an older sister, who could help with the running of the Nursery, while looking after her baby sibling.

The facilities were still very poor. There was only one room, with too many cots, a bottle room in the Pharmacy, a kitchen in Sister Elizabeth's house and a playground, near the Laundry. This created a great strain on the staff and inadequate supervision of the children. Also, the fact that they were so near to the Hospital in-patients was a source of danger, with the ever-present risk of cross-infection.

For a long time, Annette had requested funds for the Nursery and only in 1969 did she receive a donation of K10.000 (£5,000) from the Ministry of Welfare. K5000 more was now needed. She had recently received a sum of K2000 from various sources, including President Kaunda, who sent a very generous gift, the proceeds of the Senanga Church Jumble Sale and friends from Lusaka, who gave money for special equipment. Mr Simbotwe, our District Governor, who was also present at the cornerstone laying ceremony and gave his address after Annette, gave a cheque from a local club. There was also a promise of help from Livingstone Rotary Club; and the Rural Council of Senanga had put some money into the current year's estimate.

This was all very encouraging; altogether things were looking up.

The Church in Zambia and overseas expressed a great interest and was certainly praying for our needs to be supplied. A contract had already been signed with the Senanga Builders

Co-operative, which was included in the building projects of the Senanga District Development Committee.

Annette sincerely hoped the interest would flourish and that "the people of Senanga would consider the new Children's Home part of their moral and financial responsibility".

She concluded her address by expressing gratitude to all who were present and, in particular, to Sister Elizabeth, who was then on leave, for all her hard work and the Zambian staff with whom she strived to keep the children in good health.

Annette then quoted the Bible verse engraved on the entrance to the Hospital, which had been the request of two P.M.S. Missionaries, when it was first built:

"Whatever you did for one of the least important of these brothers of mine you did it for me." (Matthew 40:25)

She said, "I think, nowhere more than in the work amongst our children, this order of our Master rings true."

Annette then prayed, "May God help us day after day in this Hospital, as well as in this Children's Home, to be the servants of His wonderful love."

To this can be said a loud "AMEN"!

Chapter Forty-Six
The Haringtons' Overseas Trip

My good friends, Willie and Dinah Harrington who, incidentally were in the same age group as my parents, had now planned their World trip. Indeed, it was for them a journey of a lifetime; and they must have been among the first native Zambians to venture forth in this manner.

As soon as I knew the details of their voyage, I informed my parents of the time and date they would be landing in England, at Heathrow. I gave Willie and Dinah my parent's address in Ashford, Middlesex, which was close to the Airport; and also their telephone number.

Willie and Dinah had, sensibly, booked a hotel, for one night only, at each place throughout their tour. For their stop in London, they planned to visit my parents, which, of course, they did.

This lovely couple had been like a "mum" and "dad" to me ever since I'd arrived in Senanga. I would visit them once a fortnight and share a meal with them; Dinah was a superb cook!

Having travelled round the World; and visited the capital cities on each continent, they returned to Senanga with many wonderful memories. To my amazement and sheer delight, they told me that the highlight of their trip was meeting my parents and being invited to their home for tea.

I felt very honoured and proud of my own mum and dad!

Chapter Forty-Seven
Malaria Again!

I wasn't aware that when I had last written to my parents I must have sounded "down in the dumps". In fact, I had just recovered from a second bout of Malaria.

Of course, I made no mention of this when writing to my family, so as not to worry them unduly. But, obviously, I hadn't been able to hide the fact that I wasn't "right with the world", as they mentioned it in their letter to me. Thus, I confessed that I'd had a bad cold followed by Malaria; but was now fully recovered.

This was far from the truth: I'd had a serious chest infection with a high fever, followed, soon after, with Malaria and yet an even higher temperature, which remained for several days. I did feel ill!

Fortunately, the type of Malaria I had was not of the malignant variety; thus it would not reoccur. It just meant that I had been bitten by a mosquito carrying the virus and, as a European, my immunity to Malaria was low, unlike the indigenous African Zambian.

Although I remained in bed for only a few days, I felt weak for several weeks and lost a fair bit of weight. Luckily I had been quite robust to start with and still a healthy young woman. Otherwise I wouldn't be writing this today!

Not long after I had recovered, I had a visitor from "Tsetse Fly Control", a young man called Cliff. He was passing through Senanga; so he paid me a visit and we shared a meal together. Unfortunately, he had some sad news for me: Jock, the Scotsman, whom I have mentioned in a previous chapter, had recently died from "Blackwater Fever".

Jock had been a good friend and had very kindly taken me, together with my friends Angela and Brian, on Safari. He had also given me hospitality on my return from South Africa; so I was very upset to hear of his untimely death at the age of fifty.

Blackwater Fever is a very serious complication of Malaria, which affects the bladder, resulting in copious blood being passed in the urine; thus the apt name "Blackwater". I realised, that at the age of twenty-five, I would have had more resilience than Jock; thus I survived.

I was able to write to Jock's brother in Lusaka to which he soon replied to say he had sent my letter on to his mother in Scotland. It had given her a lot of comfort to hear what a good man her son had been.

It was the least I could do; but I am so glad I did.

I also asked the British Council to send me a mosquito net, at their earliest convenience!

Chapter Forty-Eight
Plans for the Future

During my second year in Senanga, I took an Ordinary Level G.C.E. in English Language. To my chagrin, I had twice failed this subject at school!

Although English had always been one of my best subjects; and I had even gained a prize for it at Primary School (the only one I ever had!) I hadn't been able to master "clause analysis". In other words, I knew English grammar very well; but I couldn't explain it! This was the downfall in my, otherwise, excellent progress.

Thus; I enrolled onto a correspondence course, based in London; and I quite enjoyed the studying involved. In fact, I did, eventually, come to grips with the dreaded subject of "clause analysis"!

I duly sat the examination, when attending my Medical Conference, in Lusaka, during January 1970, surrounded by African students, all of whom were male.

As I was now an "overseas" student I was required to take the exam geared to the Zambian and, therefore, African culture. This resulted in the comprehension, précis and composition having, as their main topic, a story about a "Witch Doctor" in a rural African village!

Had I not been living in the African Bush for well over a year, surrounded by typical, traditional rural culture, this would have completely "thrown" me.

However, I passed with "flying colours", gaining an "A" grade!

This was, indeed, good news, as now, armed with five "O" Levels, I could enrol at a College and study to become a Health Visitor, when I returned to England.

This was the career I was now planning to pursue; so, I began to make some tentative enquiries to the various Colleges which offered training in both theory and practice for the Health Visitor's Certificate.

Chapter Forty-Nine
A Training Weekend for Guiders and Scouters

During June 1970 I attended a weekend camp for the purpose of in-service training for Scout and Guide Leaders in Western Province (previously known as "Barotse Province").

The team consisted of Mr Kabwe, a Zambian Scout Commissioner for three Provinces, who was our organise, with him two of our P.M.S. Missionaries, Jean-Jacques, the Divisional Scout Commissioner and U.C.Z. Youth Leader and Lucette, a Secondary School Teacher, both from Switzerland and a Zambian Primary School Teacher and Scout Master.

The rest of us were a mixture of Secondary School Students, most of whom were Patrol Leaders and five Primary School Patrol Leaders, who were a mix of pupils and teachers. There were also a District Messenger, who was a Scout Leader, a School Leaver V.S.O. from England and me, who were Guide Leaders.

Altogether, there were thirty-six of us, split into four patrols of seven and one of eight. We all learned a lot and we had good fun too. We were so busy we didn't even have time to have a wash during the day!

Hence, our "baths" took place after dark, in the nearby lakes when it was very cold. After washing we swam to keep warm, which was enjoyable and definitely invigorating! Of course we had all stripped off, with the boys using one lake and us girls another. We were certainly well-organised and very clean as a result!

We ate local food, cooked on an open fire, African style with our fingers. It was delicious and I knew I would miss it when I returned home to England.

The latter proved a difficult decision, as I had a few tempting offers which would have kept me in Zambia

Mr Kabwe, a Zambian and full-time paid Scouter, encouraged me to do a District Commissioner's Course in England and then return to Zambia. The Chief Guide of Zambia had already written to me and asked me to work in Zambia, full-time in Guiding.

To top these encouraging and complimentary requests, the President of the United Church of Zambia asked me to consider medical work within the Church. Thus, I had, indeed, some important decisions to make and would need both wisdom and guidance from the Lord for the future.

I was certainly very encouraged to be asked to give my service in this way. I thanked God for the privilege of being in Zambia and having been able to make some contribution to the people here, however small it might have seemed to me.

Chapter Fifty
Plans and Decisions

By the time I was coming to the end of my two years' work in Zambia, I had made some provisional plans for the future. I had decided I would like to train as a Health Visitor, on my return to England. This was due to my experience in Senanga, where so much disease could be prevented with more health education, as well as the provision of better facilities. However, it was unlikely I would be able to begin training before September 1971, as I would need to be back home in time to attend interviews.

My other decision was how I was going to travel back to England. I had several ideas in mind, the practicality of each needing careful consideration. I was due to finish working at the Hospital at the end of August, which was six weeks from when I wrote to my parents to discuss my plans for travelling back.

I was seriously considering going by boat to Freetown, Sierra Leone, where I would stay with my good friend, Iyamide, with whom I had done my nursing training in London. Most of Iyamide's family lived in England and she was a permanent resident there. However, she was temporarily working in Sierra Leone, as a Nurse, so she could spend some time with her father, who was an Anglican Priest in Freetown.

Annette encouraged me to visit West Africa en route to England and said, "So you are even planning to hitchhike home on the boat!"

Iyamide and I wrote to each other regularly and we were looking forward very much to meeting up and then travelling back to England in time for Christmas. I was able to reassure my parents of this, although I knew they would be disappointed at not seeing me sooner. However, they wrote back and gave me their blessing.

Ironically, the day I received this letter from my parents, after several weeks of enquiry, I heard, from the travel agency in Lusaka, that there was no passage from Cape Town to Freetown, from early July till mid-November! Thus, that plan had to be scrapped.

I had already booked a flight to Livingstone for the 29th of August, which left me thirteen days to reach Cape Town for my boat back to England. Now there wouldn't be enough time to travel to Malawi and Mozambique, which I had previously considered doing.

So, I planned to travel from Livingstone via Rhodesia (now Zimbabwe) to South Africa, visiting Johannesburg and Durban en route to Cape Town. I was sorry not to be able to visit Malawi; however, Rhodesia would provide a new experience for me.

As it was still governed by Ian Smith, with his "United Declaration of Independence" (UDI) in place, VSO's were not allowed to go there while still working in Africa. However, they were permitted to visit in transit, as long as they were not returning to the countries where they worked. Incidentally, my passport wasn't stamped on arrival in Rhodesia, as I was told it would make me unpopular in England! This was a good thing really.

During July, the District Governor of Senanga asked me to take sixteen girls from my Guide Company and be a District Leader, in conjunction with sixteen "Y-teens" (a YWCA teenage group from the Copper Belt and Lusaka, led by a West Indian lady from England). They planned to come to Senanga, for two weeks, during August to do some voluntary community development work, which, in this case, was to mould clay bricks in order to build a new Rural Health Centre. This was to be located in the village of Litoya, about thirty miles from Senanga.

This work would take approximately one week, the rest of the time there being various activities and outings, including meeting President Kaunda on 17th August, when he visited Western Province.

Annette gave me her blessing for this community work, especially as it would, in the long term, improve health care for the people living at a considerable distance from the Hospital. This was as long as the other Sister (Elizabeth) had returned from leave, as it would mean me finishing work at the Hospital a week earlier than originally planned.

I hoped I would be able to catch the girls before school broke up on 7th August, as once they had returned home to their villages, it would be very difficult to get them back! I had been asked, as well, to plan evening activities, together with the other leader. I felt somewhat daunted by these extra demands; but the District Governor assured me that I would enjoy it!

He told me that he had done a lot of youth work; and had been on several courses in England. He also said that, if I wanted to return to Zambia, he would give me special recommendation to be a full-time paid Youth Worker. Yet another offer! I was overwhelmed!

Although my original plans had changed enormously, I knew being a Youth Leader, at the camp for brick making, would prove to be a far greater experience and, indeed, it was!

Chapter Fifty-One
Saying "Goodbye"

With approximately six weeks left in Senanga, I tried to pack in as much as I could in the time I had left. This included, literally, packing all the African "*objetsd,art*" I had collected over the past two years. These were carefully placed into two crates and taken in one of Willie Harrington's Lorries to Livingstone, where they were sent by airfreight to England.

This took me some considerable time, even staying up nearly two nights! However, it all arrived safely; and I had the pleasure of distributing African carvings, basketwork and woven mats as presents to my family and friends, as well as keeping a few souvenirs for myself.

I really did miss my parents, brother and sister; and I longed to see them again. The saying that "absence makes the heart grow fonder" was certainly true in my case! Thus, I was looking forward to returning to England and seeing them. However, I also knew it would be a huge wrench for me to leave Senanga and that I would feel very sad when the time came for me to leave.

The local people kept telling me that I shouldn't go and, if it was necessary, I must come back! One of my female Leprosy patients even asked me if I was going home to be married; and how much head of cattle would be given to my father by the groom!

I didn't laugh at what was, obviously, an intelligent question, from her cultural perspective. However, the thought of my father having a herd of cows in a back garden of a small house, in the outer suburbs of London, was really quite funny!

I did my best to explain the cultural differences, stating that the bride and groom would receive presents from their wedding guests; but my patient took a dim view of our customs. She considered the English bride to be compared to only a girlfriend and, therefore, not as valued or respected as the traditional Lozi bride. I had to admit that she had a good point!

Chapter Fifty-Two
Goodbye Guides

During July 1970, I took the Guides camping for the last time. It was a wonderful experience, with very mixed emotions on my part. I thoroughly enjoyed my time with these delightful young people; and they had so much to offer, both to me and to their country. I had learned such a lot from them over the past two years; and I knew I was going to miss them all very much when I left Senanga.

I took fifteen Guides with me right into the bush, about five miles from the hospital. It was a beautiful location, by the side of a lake, which was full of hippopotami; or so we were told! We didn't actually see any, although we drew our water from the lake and carried out our daily ablutions there.

We were given two lifts in the hospital Land Rover to where we would pitch our tents. One was to take our equipment with my two Patrol Leaders and myself; and the other to bring the rest of the girls.

On arrival we set to and pitched our two tents by the side of the lake. Then we proceeded to gather firewood in order to cook a meal for us all in the early evening. To my horror, I realised I had forgotten the matches! My companions soon reassured me and said, "Don't worry, Captain; we will get some fire. Just wait and see!"

The two girls then set off, returning an hour later with a piece of smouldering, dried cow dung in one of their hands! They had walked to a village about two miles away, in order to obtain the means of lighting our precious fire!

They blew on this; and in no time we had a blazing fire going, which we kept going for the whole weekend, not only for cooking, but to keep the nearby lion away during the night. We could hear them roaring, but, fortunately, didn't encounter any!

My Guides very diligently took turns in keeping the fire going all night.

These Guides would have done their founder, Lord Baden-Powell, proud. They didn't need to learn how to light a fire; neither did they need to be taught how to survive in the African Bush.

Chapter Fifty-Three
My Last Guide and Scout Campfire

On the last day of July, 1970 we held a Guide and Scout campfire at the Mission Station. This was at the end of the Term for the Secondary School, after which the students would go home to their villages until Term began again in September.

The Primary School had extended their Term till 14August, so they would be able to meet President Kaunda at Senanga Airport, when he arrived on the 11th.

This was to be my final Campfire with the Scouts and Guides of Senanga; and, as it was a special occasion, we had invited the Primary School Guides and Scouts to join us.

Naturally, I had very mixed emotions at the time. Of course, I was excited and I looked forward to what I knew would be a very enjoyable event. I had feelings of nostalgia too, as I looked back over the past two years of leading the Guides from Senanga Secondary School and developing a strong Guide Company, with dedicated and committed young girls doing their best to serve God, their president and their country.

I was very proud of my Guides; and I knew I would be very sad to say goodbye. Nevertheless, we had a wonderful time together that evening and I was determined to put my feelings aside and enjoy every moment I had with these lovely young people, belonging to the Scouts and Guides in this remote, rural area of Zambia.

I met my Guides at the Secondary School and together we marched three miles to the Mission Station, singing both Lozi and English Guide songs, which we had all learned over the past two years.

To hear these African girls singing in their own unique style was a wonderful experience in itself.

When we arrived at the Mission we met the other Scouts and Guides, and, together, we built a fire near the banks of the River Zambezi. The sun was just setting and there was a beautiful sky glowing in an amazing display of colour, such as can only be seen in this part of the world.

We continued singing, with Mubita, the Secondary School Scout Leader accompanying us on his guitar, until it was time to make the cocoa, which we did in a large iron cooking pot. We drank this in our enamel mugs, which we had all brought along, as well as eating some delicious homemade bread scones (known as "sconos" in Lozi). These had been baked earlier by the school's staff; and our appetites were well-stimulated by this time!

Finally, we all said a prayer together, sang a hymn in Lozi and ended with the Zambian National Anthem. It was a truly memorable occasion and a wonderful celebration of the friendship and unity we had built up together.

Chapter Fifty-Four
President Kaunda's Visit

11 August 1970 was a great day, when the President of Zambia visited us in Senanga. I had the honour of shaking his hand three times, once as the Guide Captain of Senanga Secondary School Guide Company, with the traditional left handshake of all Scouts and Guides and twice, in the usual manner with the right hand.

The left handshake for Scouts and Guides dated back to when Lord Baden-Powell, the founder of these movements, was in South Africa, during the Boer War. It was here that he was inspired to form what are now worldwide organisations. The idea was germinated when young "Messenger Boys" known as "Scouts", were designated to take orders, from above, to the front line.

The left handshake signified trust between the two parties, because if you intended to attack, your weapon would be in your right hand!

President Kaunda was the Chief Scout of Zambia; so it was fitting that we should observe the correct protocol on this momentous occasion! I wrote to my parents that I now wouldn't be able to wash either hand! It was, indeed, a great privilege to have met the President in this way.

The Scouts and Guides of Senanga's two Primary Schools with me and the two Scoutmasters were on parade, proudly holding their flags and staves, in a space, on the outside of the barrier, where the president's plane would land. Others, who were allowed in, were the local chiefs, village headmen, and U.N.I.P. (United Independence Party) officials, heads of departments (including Annette, our Doctor and Rene the Church Minister), the District Governor and the Melena Mukwai (Chief Princess and daughter of the late Paramount Chief).

The President arrived, by plane, at 10:30 am. We had been standing since 7:30 am; but there had been a change in the programme! We had certainly been faithful to the Scout and Guide motto – "Be Prepared!"

The President then proceeded to shake hands with the aforementioned people, including myself and the two Scout Leaders; and he saluted us in his role of Chief Scout Commissioner. It was a proud moment for us all.

Unfortunately, the Guides and Scouts from the Secondary School were absent, having all gone away on holiday!

When the President addressed the crowd, he was directly in front of us. He gave a fine speech with a deep Christian message. Indeed, it would have made an excellent sermon! He emphasised the importance of all the tribes and the different ethnic groups being united and creating a nation of people, equal in the eyes of God.

I took quite a few photos; and one of the Scout Leaders took one of me shaking hands with the President. It was a momentous occasion.

In the afternoon, President Kaunda visited the Hospital. The staff stood outside and we sung a hymn in Lozi, in which the President joined in, singing in his own tribal language of Bemba. It was a very moving moment.

Afterwards, the Sisters, Medical Assistant and Senior Dressers were introduced to him. Then he visited all the Wards and Departments. When he left the Hospital, I happened to be at the entrance; so he shook my hand again and said "goodbye". By now we had become firm friends!

President Kaunda was a fine looking man and commanded awe and respect. His English was very good, with a cultured accent; but the people of Senanga were delighted that he had initially greeted them in Lozi. It was the first time he had visited our Hospital; so you can imagine just how excited we all were.

Over the past week we had all been extremely busy making preparations and cleaning the place up. Annette said that even if he didn't come then at least the Hospital would be a lot cleaner!

As it happened, he did come; so our labour was not in vain; and our efforts were rewarded with an occasion none of us would ever forget.

Chapter Fifty-Five
Brick Making in Litoya

On 13 August 1970, having finished working at the Hospital the previous day, I travelled to Mongu to meet the team of girls from the Copper Belt and their Leader. The following day we all met President Kaunda. This was to be my third time; and, indeed, it was a great privilege and one none of us would ever forget. For me, it was like meeting an old friend again.

The President showed a keen interest in the work we were going to be involved in, which was that of making bricks, in order to build a new Health Centre in a remote, rural area of Senanga District, in the renamed Western Province (originally known as Barotseland, the home of the Lozi tribe).

President Kaunda was a strong advocate of Preventative Medicine and his government was promoting Health Education throughout Zambia.

At the time I wrote to my parents, I was experiencing great difficulty in getting the girls I needed for my team. The end of Term for the Senanga Secondary School was 7th August and the pupils, including most my Guides, quite naturally, wanted to go home.

Where we would be working, making bricks in Litoya Village, was a long way from where these girls lived and it would be nigh on impossible for them to return, once they left the School.

I now hoped to be able to build my team from the upper grades of Senanga Primary School, which was staying open for the President's visit. The age group required was fifteen to eighteen year olds, of which there were many still receiving Primary educations. However, these girls didn't mix as easily as the Secondary School girls, mainly due to lack of experience, and thus, confidence.

My plan was to visit them at the School and encourage them to take part in such an important Community venture. Also, these girls nearly all lived in Senanga; so it would be easy to provide transport for them to Litoya. In fact, they would be able to travel with me as their Leader.

Mary, the Teacher from the Primary School, who helped me with my Guide Company whilst Fabia was on maternity leave, was of great assistance. Together, with her brother, the Primary School Scout Leader and also a teacher, she helped me to recruit a team of Primary School Guides to attend the "Brick Making Camp", as we now called it.

On Friday, 14th August, I met the twelve girls, from the Copper belt, at the Mission station where the Primary School was situated. They had travelled from Mongu earlier that day. Here they stayed until we all travelled to Litoya on the Monday (17th August).

I had succeeded in getting eight girls from the Primary School and we all spent a wonderful weekend together in Senanga.

In the evening, the District Governor held a party for us at his house, which we all enjoyed and it gave us a chance to get to know each other.

On Saturday, we all had the privilege of visiting the Mulena Mukwai (Chief Princess of the Lozi Tribe) at her Palace in a village, a few miles away. On Sunday we went to Church at the Mission Station, where Rene Arriege, the Pastor, preached a fine sermon, which was a great encouragement to us as we prepared to spend several days in a remote village, making clay bricks during the heat of the day.

After Church we had a splendid meal in the garden outside. Later on, once our dinner was digested, we went swimming in the River Zambezi, close by! We also had the chance to paddle a traditional "dugout" canoe, which was great fun. The girls did very well, including those from the Copper Belt who didn't usually have this opportunity.

To complete this relaxing and enjoyable weekend we visited Litambya Village, close to the Hospital and joined in some traditional dancing with the local people.

We certainly gave our visitors a good time in Senanga!

On Monday, 17th August, we set off in two Land Rovers to travel thirty miles to Litoya, where we spent nine days making the bricks. I had eight girls in my team and we stayed together in one tent, while the girls from the Copper Belt were in another tent with their leader, whose name was Rosemary.

Rosemary was originally from Barbados, and was now a resident of London. She had come to Zambia as a Youth Leader, employed by the British Ministry of Overseas Development, to work in Zambia for three years on a contract. Most of her work was in the urban areas; so this was a very new experience for her.

As for me, I was now quite a "seasoned" adopted rural "Zambian", having worked at the Hospital and with the Guides for two years in Senanga.

It was hard work making the clay bricks, especially in the heat of the day, which, even for the African girls, was uncomfortable. We would all have to cover up well to avoid being sunburnt. However, we had a great time together and found it very rewarding.

The men would dig the clay and we moulded the bricks, which were then sent off to be baked in a special oven.

We lived just like the local people, only we slept in tents and not mud huts. We cooked all our meals in black iron pots, on an open fire and ate a simple diet of cassava, sweet potato and mealie-meal, together with fish from a nearby lake and locally grown vegetables. We drew our water from a well, dug out on the plain and I learned to carry a bucket on my head!

Twice a week we went to the lake in the forest, two miles away, to have a good wash, which we always badly needed after working with clay in the hot sun several hours a day! The rest of the time we would wash ourselves and our clothes at the well, with the other women.

I also ran a clinic for the local people, twice a day. Luckily I had a medical kit with me, which I hardly had to use for the Brick Making Team. However, I was able to put it to good use, without my supply running out.

Mostly, I treated Malaria, snakebites and minor wounds and injuries. For anything more serious I authorised transport to the Hospital, when it became available.

I didn't realise how well known I was in these parts. I even discovered the local mothers were naming their baby girls

"Janet", after me! I had delivered many of these babies at the Hospital. I felt quite humbled and very privileged indeed.

When it was time for us all to leave Litoya, the whole village came out and thanked me, personally, for what I had done. Although very gratified, I felt quite sad too, as the time for me to leave these dear people was rapidly approaching.

Of course, the villagers were also very grateful to all of us for making the bricks. Certainly, my experience of running a very makeshift clinic highlighted their urgent need of a purpose-built Health Centre, staffed by suitably qualified Health Workers. Thus, these people living in such a remote area, far from the Hospital, could be given the care they needed.

Working in Litoya had been a wonderful experience; and I knew I would never forget the time I spent there.

Chapter Fifty-Six
Travel Plans

By the time I'd arrived back to Senanga on 26th August, I'd still not received my tickets for the boat from Cape Town to Tilbury. However, there was a letter from the Travel Agency in Lusaka, containing a form for me to complete and state whether I wanted the tickets posted to Senanga, or would I prefer to collect them in Cape Town. As I was leaving Senanga at the end of the month, this was a bit late in the day!

I duly filled in the form and requested them to send my tickets directly to Cape Town, "Immediately!" Senanga Mission Station also agreed to radio a message to the United Church of Zambia's Headquarters in Lusaka and tell them the same. With no Internet this was the best we could do to expedite matters!

With a bit of luck, my letter would catch Saturday's plane in two days' time! Fortunately it did; and, eventually, I collected my tickets in Cape Town. All was well!

My plan for travelling down to South Africa was to include visiting friends and family, "en route".

Therefore, I wrote to everyone I planned to see. I sent these letters several weeks before I left the Hospital. Despite my unconventional method of travel, hitchhiking from Rhodesia, via Bulawayo, all the way to Cape Town, I arrived at each destination at approximately, the expected time!

More about this epic journey in a later chapter!

Chapter Fifty-Seven
Farewell Senanga!

I arrived back to Senanga from Litoya very brown and very dirty! On arrival at our house, Annette told me that there was no hot water, as her bathroom was being repaired. This didn't present a problem for me. I told Annette that I was quite happy to go down to the river and wash with the women and girls there, as this is what I had been doing for the past two weeks!

This I did promptly, as my need for a good wash was very necessary; and, I do believe, Annette thought the same! The women accepted me readily, although they did think it unusual for a white person to do the same as them, as they knew we had more modern facilities than they did.

However, they were very happy for me to join them and share my soap, which I readily lent them. Also, the young girls were delighted to swim with me – the only time they dared venture out in the middle of the river!

All this was a very special memory of my last few days in Senanga and an occasion I would never forget.

The girls from the Copper Belt, as well as my own team of Guides from Senanga, stayed at the Primary School for the next two days, with a party planned for us all the following evening.

Such an event was not just a celebration of our shared experience of being part of an important Community Project and the strong bond of friendship we developed; but it was also a sad time when we all said "goodbye" to one another. All this was preparing me for leaving Senanga in a few days' time.

My friends, Willie and Dinah Harrington, had only just returned from their World Trip and I hadn't had a chance to see them since. This would be a sad farewell. I had known this lovely family ever since arriving in Senanga in August, 1968, and they had embraced me as one of their own. I knew I was going to miss them very much, indeed.

With this being my first visit to Willie and Dinah since they had returned, it was a case of "hello" and "goodbye". I did, however, spend a very pleasant evening, with a splendid meal having been prepared for me. We shared fond memories, reminisced and it turned out to be a joyful occasion, after all.

There would always be mixed emotions of nostalgia, joy and sadness whenever I remembered the friends I had made in Zambia; and these would last forever, at least for as long as I lived!

My packing was almost at the last minute. I think this must have reflected my reluctance to leave my life in Senanga behind. Nevertheless, it had to be done.

Taulo, my "good and faithful servant" did all my washing and ironing, bless him. I then packed my clothes, which consisted of cotton dresses, underwear and just a few other "bits and pieces". These went into one small suitcase; so it didn't take too long and I was ready for the road!

The day I returned from brick making in Litoya, I went across to the Hospital to say "hello" to my patients and the staff, whom I hadn't seen for two weeks. I was given a very warm welcome by them all. I could hardly believe I would be leaving in three days and saying "goodbye"!

I knew this would be difficult; and, indeed, it was!

The evening before I left Senanga, I was invited to a meal with Anna and Pumulo, our two Maternity Assistants, who my predecessor, Ann, had trained as Midwives. They cooked a delicious, traditional Lozi meal of "buhobe" (ground maize meal, otherwise known as "mealie meal") and fish, fresh from the Zambesi. Of course we ate with our fingers, which is really the only way to eat such food; and is most enjoyable.

On 26th August I wrote my last letter from Senanga to my parents. In it I said that I had got so used to Zambian cuisine that I was really going to miss it when I returned to England.

I spent a very pleasant evening with Anna and Pumulo, who both spoke good English and were in the same age group as myself. I believe it was the first time they had entertained an English person in their home and, indeed, any "Westerner".

I felt quite honoured to be their guest as I think they did, for me to have visited them in their traditional African home, made from mud and thatch. This would be forever, another treasured memory.

On the day I left Senanga (Saturday, 29th September) Annette drove me in the Hospital Land Rover to the Airport (really only a strip of land, just large enough for a thirty-two seater Dakota to land and take off).

I wept "buckets" of tears all the way! It was a journey of four miles and took us roughly twenty minutes. Annette did her very best to console me, but to no avail! I learned many years later, that when Annette finally retired and left Senanga, she was in much the same state.

When we reached the Airport, nearly all the staff from the hospital was there to say "goodbye", both African and European. Even faithful Taulo, who had walked barefoot all the way, carrying two woven African mats for me to take home. I think he genuinely believed I would need these to sleep on, during my long journey!

As I took my seat, at the back of the plane, I saw him giving the mats to the Pilot to put in the hold, saying in Lozi, these belong to "Bo Missy". I couldn't control my emotions any more. I just broke down and cried all the way to Livingstone!

Later, during the journey, I was visited by a Dutch Church Minister, who was travelling, with Rene, to a U.C.Z. conference in Lusaka. Rene must have sent him to me or, maybe' it was the Lord, Himself! For this kind, Christian gentleman came and sat beside me, holding my hand and speaking words of comfort.

What he said will always stick in my mind: "You must have truly loved these people". And I realised I did!

Chapter Fifty-Eight
My Journey Home

Part One

"Goodbye Africa"

I wrote my last letter to my parents from the African Continent, on 10th September, 1970. In it I described my journey from Senanga down to Cape Town, where I boarded a boat heading for England, my home.

Of course, I said how much I was looking forward to seeing them all, i.e., my parents, brother, Jeffrey and his fiancée, Margaret, and my "little sister", Stella.

My journey took me by plane from Senanga, three hundred miles, to Livingstone. Here I stayed with David, a Methodist Minister from England. I had already met David and his family when he visited us on his arrival in Zambia, a few months earlier; so I felt quite at home with them all.

David had been sent by the Methodist Missionary Society and was now working with the United Church of Zambia, in Livingstone.

I spent a pleasant weekend there, visiting the Victoria Falls for the second time – a truly amazing sight – and seeing also some traditional dancing, which was quite spectacular.

Whilst there, I was able to sort out the business of sending my luggage, which had already been transported from Senanga in one of Willie Harrington's Lorries. I did this by Air Freight, as to send it by road might have taken too long; and it would have missed the boat, literally!

It was only a little more expensive; and certainly it was a lot safer than it going through Rhodesia. Eventually, we were able to pick it up at London Airport, close by my parent's home, in

Ashford. After collecting such African "treasures", I thanked God for their safe arrival!

I set off from Livingstone on Tuesday, 1st September and hitchhiked to Johannesburg, via Bulawayo. The latter proved to be an interesting experience although, for me, somewhat uncomfortable. Whereas in South Africa "Apartheid" was fundamentally wrong, it didn't always reflect racist attitudes. A lot of the problem was fostered by the separate existence of the major ethnic groups, lack of education and ignorance.

This situation also prevailed in Northern Ireland, through the two communities of "Protestants" and "Catholics" living apart and going to separate schools; thus never really getting to know one another. For the minority, who went onto Higher Education these problems were often "ironed out".

What I experienced in Bulawayo, where I stayed overnight in a hotel, was outright racism. Here I found myself hearing inflammatory statements and insults against the Africans, such as I had never heard on all my travels throughout South Africa.

Both the Landlord and his wife had lived in Northern Rhodesia before Independence and, now, they were highly critical of the country and it's Government. I made the comment that, during the Colonial regime there was just one Secondary School, which only a few privileged Africans could attend. Now, due to President Kaunda and his Government, there was one in each district of Zambia – a country eight times the size of England.

I also emphasised that the Africans needed good education to be able to run the country; and this was, at last, available, and I, for one, wished them every success. They were unable to argue with what I said!

I also engaged in another conversation with two white South African men, who told me the tale of a white person going to a clairvoyant in search of a long-lost relation. In the same breath, they described the "typical", African as being ignorant, because it was common practice for them to consult a "witch doctor", when requiring supernatural knowledge.

Again I got myself into trouble when I questioned as to what was the difference between these two approaches. As far as I was concerned, there was very little. In fact, the white person would have had the opportunity for a good education, whereas, in most cases, the majority of Africans, living in traditional rural areas, would not. I certainly gave them food for thought!

When I arrived in Johannesburg, I discovered my cousin, Vivian, had already left for England, apparently quite suddenly. Her good friend, Peter, very kindly accommodated me overnight in his spacious flat. He was the perfect gentleman and took me out for a delicious meal that evening. The next day he secured a lift for me to Pietermaritzburg, where I stopped with Marie and her family.

I had known Marie, who had lived in Senanga with her husband, for the past two years and we had become good friends. Unfortunately, their marriage had failed and she had been in South Africa for a few months. Marie was delighted to see me again, and I was made very welcome by her daughter, Christine and her family.

From Pietermaritzburg I travelled to Durban, where I stayed with my "Uncle" Bill and "Aunty" Cath. It was lovely to see them again and my two cousins, David and Dianne. I promised Uncle Bill that I would visit his mother, my Great Aunty Carrie, when I returned home.

Not only did I keep my promise and visit Aunty Carrie in Brentford, Middlesex, a month later; but, at the same time, Dianne was there too! This was, indeed, a very happy occasion!

From Durban, in Natal, I travelled south, via Port Elizabeth, to Belleville, a small town in Cape Province, not far from Cape Town. I stayed here with my friend Jenia's mother. I really enjoyed seeing her again, as we had got on so well on my last visit in 1969. Two days later I went to Cape Town, where I had a meal with Jenia and her family before setting off to the dock, with her husband, Tony, driving us there.

Jenia, by this time, was expecting her third child in two weeks! She accompanied me as far as the boat, together with her two children, Lavinia, aged four, and Anthony aged two. My last view of Africa was of the three of them waving goodbye, with a backdrop of the majestic Table Mountain.

I wondered whether I would ever see it again! This was a very nostalgic moment; and I stood on deck until I could see land no more.

Part Two
"Ocean Bound"

I spent sixteen days on a Merchant Navy Liner, owned by Ellerman and Bucknall Shipping Company. For me, I was in the "lap of luxury" on what was a cruise half way round the World.

The food was fantastic! I had never eaten some of the meals served on board and I felt thoroughly spoilt. Everything was "on the house" although, of course, it had all been paid for. V.S.O. had made a substantial contribution; but I had to subsidise the cost, as a flight would have cost a lot less.

Each evening, there was ballroom dancing and I never had to wait too long to be asked to dance! I wasn't really very good at this kind of dancing; but the men with whom I danced were; and they were able to lead me. I soon improved and ended up enjoying these dances very much.

Most of the people on board were over sixty and enjoying a well-earned cruise in their retirement. The other "young" people, apart from me and the crew, included a women of thirty-five, called Susan, with her two daughters of nine and eleven years of age, a young lad of fifteen, who was travelling with his parents, who worked for the British Government; and a teacher, the same age as myself, called Bob, from Bolton.

I made great friends with Susan and we would spend a lot of time swimming in the pool on deck each day. Bob always invited me to have a drink with him in the evening; but he was hopeless at dancing!

On two occasions I was invited to sit at the Captain's Table, at our evening meal; and this was considered a great honour.

There was a retired Anglican Clergyman on board; so Susan and I asked if he would celebrate Holy Communion each morning, to which he gladly complied. He was very encouraged by a good number of us attending.

Each Sunday the Captain conducted a morning Service of Christian worship, which all the crew attended and several passengers. It was quite impressive to see the crew so smart in their uniforms, standing reverently, with their caps off.

There were also film shows and for the first time, I watched "Butch Cassidy and the Sundance Kid," starring Paul Newman and Robert Redford and thoroughly enjoyed it.

After a week of such luxury, the novelty began to wear off and I longed to be home and see my family. I really didn't want to have to wait over another week. I also missed Africa, my life in the Bush and a much more simple way of life.

Crossing the Equator was an experience; and I was duly dipped in the pool by "King Neptune" and given a certificate. It was quite fun really, with Susan and her daughters joining in too.

Towards the end of our journey we docked at Southend for our last night. This was our first stop other than the one at Palma, in the Canaries. We weren't able to continue up the Thames to Tilbury until the following morning when it would be high tide again.

On the last night a party was held by the crew to which I was duly invited, along with a few others. It was quite a "wild" affair, with plenty of loud music, more modern dancing than the traditional ballroom; and, there was plenty to eat and drink. Although, by today's standards it was probably fairly tame!

I enjoyed myself to a certain extent; but I missed the African dancing and music I had become accustomed to. Indeed, I was beginning to experience "culture shock" in reverse!

Finally, our journey ended in Tilbury Dock, on Sunday, 7th September, 1970; and there I met my parents, brother and sister. I also met my brother's fiancée, Margaret for the first time.

I didn't know what to expect; but I know when I saw them we all cried, hugged and kissed one another. It was wonderful to be reunited with my family once again. I realised just how much I loved them all; and I was overjoyed to see them after such a long time.

Afterword

On my return to England I really did experience "culture shock". There couldn't have been a greater contrast than that of London, where I had previously lived all my life, and rural Africa.

Travelling on the Underground and the pace of City life, was quite overwhelming. However, I was comforted by the presence of so many ethnic minorities and the cosmopolitan atmosphere of London.

It was good to be reunited with all my family and friends; but very few could really understand the experience I'd had in Zambia.

I spent a weekend with Jo, a returned V.S.O. Nurse and Midwife from an Anglican Mission, in Zambia, at her parent's home in Kent. We were of a kindred spirit and it was good to see her again.

I also stayed with Ann, my predecessor in Senanga. She lived in London and we spent a weekend together reminiscing and catching up on latest news of our mutual friends and colleagues.

One of the African U.C.Z. Ministers was attending a Church Conference in London; and he contacted me so we could arrange to meet each other. Whilst visiting this gentleman I was introduced to a young Zambian called Oscar. He was from the Copper Belt and had recently arrived in London to train as a Public Health Inspector.

Oscar and I became great friends; I was able to show him the sights of London and he was a very reliable escort.

I also spent many a weekend with my friend Iyamide's family, her mother, brothers and sisters, living in Bow in London's East End. This lovely Christian family always gave me a warm welcome and I became part of the family.

Although I did, at first, find it hard to settle, once I had embarked on my Health Visitor's training at the North East London Polytechnic, I began to settle down.

It really was quite Providential that I was able, after all, to start this intensive one year course in October, 1970, just a month since returning to England. The Principal Health Visitor Tutor, Miss Lynch, had written to me in Senanga, the letter arriving after I had set off for my journey home!

However, eventually I received the letter, which requested me to contact her as soon as I had returned. I did this during October, was interviewed and accepted on the Course! This was, indeed, an answer to prayer, as everyone else had started in September.

I thoroughly enjoyed my studies as well as the practical experience I gained; and qualified as a Health Visitor in October 1971.

I was sponsored by the London Borough of Tower Hamlets for the College Course and, having passed all the written exams, I went to work in Poplar for two years.

Thus, I found myself working with indigenous Cockney families, as well as immigrants from the West Indies and Asia.

I did not know then how well-known Poplar would become as a result of "Call the Midwife". More than likely, the young mothers I visited were the "babies" delivered by Jennifer Worth and her colleagues!

I never did go back to work overseas; but my career as a Health Visitor in London was both very rewarding as well as challenging.